D0232946

The Capers Papers

The Capers Papers

By **Charlotte Capers**

Foreword by Eudora Welty

UNIVERSITY PRESS OF MISSISSIPPI
Jackson

Copyright © 1982 by Charlotte Capers
All Rights Reserved
Manufactured in the United States of America
Designed by Barney McKee

First Printing, March 1982
Second Printing, July 1982
Third Printing, January 1983

Library of Congress Cataloging in Publication Data

Capers, Charlotte.
    The Capers papers.

    Selections from the author's columns in the
Jackson daily news, the Jackson state times, and
the Delta review.
    I. Title.
AC8.C1822 1982   081   81-22013
ISBN 0-87805-152-X   AACR2

All of the material in this book, except the piece on Allison's
Wells, appeared originally under the standing head "Miss
Quote" in the *Jackson Daily News,* the standing head "Miss
Quote" and my byline in the *Jackson State Times,* and the
standing head "The Good Life" in *The Delta Review.* I am
grateful to Mr. Tom Hederman, president of the Mississippi Publishing Company, Inc., for his kind permission to
reprint the columns which appeared originally in the *Jackson Daily News,* and to Hosford Fontaine for her kind permission to reprint the introduction to her book *Allison's
Wells: The Last Mississippi Spa* published in December,
1981.   C.C.

To the Memory of My Grandmother,
Eliza Keesee Woldridge

Contents

Foreword by Eudora Welty   9

Author's Note   12

God and My Grandmother   13

   God and My Grandmother   15

Pass the Pesticide, Pappy   29

   Pass the Pesticide, Pappy   31

   Ivy League   34

   My Dog Holly   36

   Moving Day   42

   Wreck   44

   Not Speaking of Operations   48

The Pain of It All   53

   The Pain of It All   55

   Be It Ever So   58

   Queen of the May   62

   Tell Me About Your Trip   64

   Good Sport   66

   Planning to Build?   68

   There Go the Joneses   70

Apartment for Rent   73

  Apartment for Rent   75

  Tiny Tenant   80

  By the Dawn's Early Light   81

  How to Get a Baby   83

  The Little Wrecker   84

  La Mere Goose   86

  Out of the Nowhere   88

  Summer is for Children   91

Fasten Your Seat Belts   95

  What, la Peste?   97

  Fasten Your Seat Belts   98

  Westward the Women   107

  Pawley's Island   110

  Allison's Wells   117

  Autumn Light   120

Foreword

by Eudora Welty

CHARLOTTE CAPERS NEVER thought to collect her papers. Her colleagues in the Archives have now done it for her, making their choices from a large number that go back for several decades. Here they are for our delight.

We will all have to agree at once to this: they represent Charlotte but they cannot convey her. They weren't written with that in mind, for they came about by circumstance. Many of them—some of the best, in fact—are samples of her warmly remembered Sunday newspaper column, "Miss Quote," set down spontaneously in response to an occasion. The occasion would have been local; it might have been of public or personal import, might have been anything that flagged the author down as she came its way or it came hers. They were crowded by space limitations and pressed by the deadline, but they were tossed off with ease and speed. And they acutely reflected their day. They can still call it up, and remind us well that Charlotte Capers never missed a thing in the passing scene.

She's such a part of it herself. Charlotte does a variety of things well and enthusiastically besides write. She'd rather rise up and dance than sit down and type. She favors the spontaneous, she enjoys the immediate response, the give-and-take of conversation, in which she is a virtuoso. Writing is something you do by yourself. This is the most serious strike against it, or Charlotte may jokingly let you think that; but in the judgment of another writer who has kept urging her on, she writes entirely too well not to take an honest satisfaction from doing it. When we read the collection here we want still more.

Most of these pieces were written to amuse, and they abundantly do so. If some of them are fleeting, so was, and so is, the passing scene. The point is that Charlotte *caught* something. Her perceptions are not only quick and bright but accurate and wise. She knows her world. She sees the social world we all move in with its history behind it, too, that built and shaped, and sometimes shadowed, our times. She is a viewer with perspective.

It is above all, though, the sense of people, of human nature and intractable human behavior that intrigues and stirs and delights her mind, and fairly often confirms her expectations. It's the rest of us that set her off. Herself too she can take on as an equally qualified subject; her own adventures make her best pieces. Her writing might spring out of that sensitivity to human idiosyncrasy which very often brings about such a satisfactory evening of conversation between friends. (*Southern* conversation, as we know and practice it.)

They are wonderfully conversational, these flowing pieces. However she makes it appear, the conversational style is not at all easy to get down on paper. Charlotte has mastered her style without seeming to try; this is characteristic of her. The Capers style, in her papers as in her character, is intuitive, receptive, hospitable, unpredictable but *succinct*.

To relish human nature (which is a talent all its own—you probably have to be born with it) is to pretty well know it, to be well-prepared and seasoned to its surprises and revelations. She applies the extravagant idiom, the outrageous now and then: it offers her a reasonable amount of scope in a small column of type, and comes in generally handy for reporting what goes on here. Exaggeration is one of her splendid accomplishments. Just as a towering skyscraper can only be built on bed rock that goes deep and stands unquivering, to exaggerate as tellingly as Charlotte can, you need to be pretty firmly based in human truths.

These pieces vary in subject and mood and kind. But they convey in common a warmth of feeling you won't fail to recognize as Charlotte's own. In reading the Capers papers we hear the Capers voice.

The beautifully written "God and My Grandmother," an essay given the full development it deserves, has the power to deeply stir us. "Pawley's Island" is a sensitive and very special evocation of a place. The exemplary portrait of the "Tiny Tenant" is made up of one part clear eyed observation, one part headlong devotion, and no part whatever of sentimentality. You will decide which are your own favorites. In any case, the last piece, "Autumn Light," an elegy of our state in 1954, is likely to remain a picture in all our minds, not fleeting but indelible.

Eudora Welty

Author's Note

THESE PIECES WERE written in the fifties, the sixties, and the seventies, when I was an occasional columnist for the *Jackson Daily News*, the *Jackson State Times*, and the *Delta Review*. The columns were clipped as they appeared, and relegated to the files of the Mississippi Department of Archives and History. Here they reposed until my colleagues, Chrissy Wilson and Patti Black, exhumed them from the files and decided that they would make a book. I am innocent of their plotting but grateful for it. I am also grateful to Mary Mingee for typing the columns over and over and laughing occasionally, and to Ann Morrison for producing the Tiny Tenant and helping with selections. Elbert Hilliard, director of the Department of Archives and History, and the members of the Board of Trustees of the Department of Archives and History, thought well of the project and gave it their full support. I deeply appreciate all of this, but most of all I appreciate the friendship of the people with whom I have worked for so many years.

Charlotte Capers

 God and My Grandmother

God and My Grandmother

WHEN MOTHER AND I got to Columbia every summer, Grandmother would be on the front porch, waving and crying. The crying was because she was so happy to see us. If she had not been crying, I would have been disappointed.

We usually left Jackson for Columbia the last week in June, and Father joined us in August if nobody in the congregation at St. Andrew's was seriously sick. Somebody was always sick, as I remember it, and it seemed to me that all Episcopalians appointed to die did so in August. As pastor, Father saw his sheep in or out of the Valley of the Shadow, and thus was often late for his vacation. Mother and I went on ahead, and had most of the summer in Columbia, Tennessee, where her parents lived.

When I was nine or ten Columbia was heaven to me. This attitude was due in large part to Grandmother, who was in close touch with the Almighty and made heaven seem a very attractive place.

Our summer pleasure began when Moses met us at the C.M.A. station in the old Essex, and drove us home. My grandparents lived in a two-story brick house on the

Mt. Pleasant Pike. The house, built in the 1880s, was late Victorian in style, and was set far back from the Pike. A gravel driveway led through stone gate-posts to the house. It had a fine tin roof, on which the rain drummed marvelously. It had a cupola, with a lightning rod rampant. And it had heavy wooden shutters at the windows, which were closed every afternoon at nap-time by Moses, with the aid of a broom-handle with a hook on the end of it. The shutters were closed from the outside, of course, and they were very effective. I remember the dim cool of the library, produced almost the instant the shutters closed. The front door was half-glass, at the top, framed in little squares of stained glass.

Middle Tennessee had more than its share of rip-roaring windstorms and thunder storms, and when a storm was brewing, Grandmother and I would go to the front door and watch the trees toss wildly in the wind. Grandmother would tell me about storms that blew cows up into trees, and houses off their foundations. We looked at the storm through the red glass and the blue glass and the yellow glass, and this gave a weird, other-worldly glow to the scene as the trees bent to the wind and the lightning flashed. The limbs twisted and snapped, and sometimes there was a tearing, cracking noise as a tree went down. Then Grandmother and I would dash from the front door and take refuge in the bathroom, which for some reason she thought was saf-est in storms.

This bathroom had been added on with the advent of plumbing, and it was a funny little room painted bathroom blue and smelling of strong blue carbolic acid soap. The pipes made strange sounds when the water was drained out of the wash basin, and one of the Negroes had told my brother that this was the plumber, coming to get him. He passed this bit of folklore down to me, and I was really more frightened of the bathroom than I was of the storm, when the gurgling of the pursuing plumber was heard in the pipes.

Anyway, Grandmother and I huddled in the bathroom and she prayed until the storm passed. Grandmother was very religious, and I thought she always had been. But Father said, "No, she took a turn in her early married life when some evangelist came to town." Before that she had been an Episcopalian in a relaxed sort of a way, but the evangelist really got to her. She didn't leave the Episcopal Church, but she tightened up on some sins that hadn't worried her before. She made Granddaddy stop betting on harness races, and when Uncle Stith, Granddaddy's younger brother, made the long trip from Brooklyn, New York, to visit them, she found a bottle of whisky in his room and forthwith poured it down the toilet. Uncle Stith never returned, understandably enough, and Grandmother's religious turn continued to her life's end.

By the time I was old enough to hear and receive the Word, Grandmother had mellowed considerably, but I still got a stiff course in the Bible every summer. We had Bible reading every morning, and Grandmother was such a good reader I looked forward to these sessions, as well as to Family Prayer at night. I knew also that I had to read the Bible before I rode the pony, and I accepted this sequence of events as Virtue and Its Own Reward. I could not ride until Joshua had fought the battle of Jericho, or made the sun stand still. When I was excused by Grandmother and left for the latticed back porch and the pony standing hitched to the acting bar in the back yard, I was often worried about what was going to happen to Joshua next.

There were no children near to play with, so the days were pretty much spent in reading and horseback riding, and sometimes croquet with the grown people in the late afternoon. At night we had Family Prayer, and Grandmother was in charge of this operation, too. After she and Granddaddy had played checkers or euchre or High-Low-Jack in the library, and Father and Mother had come in from supper with friends or the picture show, and the grown people had run through a game of riddles or conundrums with me, it was time for Family Prayer. We had it from the Prayer Book, and we had Evening straight through. Then if there were any special problems, we did Additional Prayers to cover them.

Additional Prayers were usually for my brother, Walter, who was sixteen or seventeen and seemed to be always standing in the need of prayer. He was full of all sorts of natural juices, and he had discovered Nashville, forty miles away, and girls. So he was not with us much at night, but Grandmother always remembered him in our prayers. She prayed for him to be healed of whatever accident had recently befallen him. I remember one summer we prayed for Walter's foot, when he cut it with an axe, and we prayed for his head, when he jumped a horse over a stone fence and was thrown, and we prayed for him to recover from typhoid fever, which he contracted at summer camp. We also prayed regularly for him to get home from Nashville safely. In the mornings we did not see him, for he was asleep. Grandmother spoke of him as King Agrippa—I don't know why unless it was because Herod Agrippa was such a high-riding king, and Grandmother's orientation was so Biblical. She would say, "Sh-h, King Agrippa's still asleep," and everyone would tip-toe around and sympathize with the poor tired boy who had danced all night.

Walter was very charming and pretty spoiled, and Father complained about it a good deal. "These women are ruining Walter," he would say. "They won't let me make him work." They really wouldn't, because Walter was so good-looking and so polite, and wherever my mother and Grandmother went ladies told them that he was Prince Charming and Lord Chesterfield, and they believed them. Add King Agrippa to this, and he could have been a real mess, but somehow he wasn't. In the winter Father tried without success to get Walter to help around the house, and he would say, "I can bring the coal in and make the fires without losing my religion, but I cannot make Walter bring the coal in and make the fires without losing my religion." Which is to say that Walter was seventeen, and I did not see much of him in the summer.

When special supplications or additional prayers were over, we had the Aaronic blessing. Grandmother preferred this one to "the grace of our Lord Jesus Christ, the love of God, and the fellowship of the Holy Ghost," though she was all for the Trinity. Aaron is said to have said, "The Lord bless us and keep us. The Lord make his face to shine upon us and be gracious unto us. The Lord lift up his countenance upon us, and give us peace, both now and evermore." I liked that too, not for any special reason or because we were stronger on the Old Testament, but because the words were so pretty.

When the blessing was said Grandmother kissed Granddaddy on the cheek and said, "God bless you, Mr. Woldridge," and Granddaddy kissed Grandmother on the cheek and said, "God bless you, Miss Liza," and we all went to bed. I got to sleep in Grandmother's room.

She had a white iron single bed put up beside her bed, next to the old walnut wardrobe. When I had bad dreams I thought the heavy old wardrobe was a monster. I have seen ghosts come out of it, as a door creaked heavily open on its hinges. Before we went to sleep we named all of the oceans of the world, and we imagined a voyage on one of them which we were to describe to each other the next morning. We named the corners of the room for sweethearts, of which I had none, and the corners of the bed for saints.

Then Grandmother might be moved to tell me about the beaux she had before she married Granddaddy, or of the little baby whose crib stood in the corner of that very room, who died before she was six weeks old, or of the visions she had seen. Father would have thought she was crazy, so I never discussed the visions with him. But Grandmother told of climbing a high white mountain, with mists swirling about the top, and stumbling, and falling back, and stumbling again, and falling back, and being about to plunge to the rocky depths below, and then a hand, which was the hand of God, reached out from the top of the mountain, through the mists, and clasped her hand, and brought her home. I thought this was a very nice vision, and it was Grandmother's type.

She liked her religion dramatic and she was High Church, as opposed to Father, who was Low. Grandmother liked everything mystical, and all the bells and incense and genuflections in the world would not have seemed too much to her, to worship the King, all glorious above. Father, on the other hand, was a South Carolina low country low churchman, and he had gone to Seminary in Virginia besides. He had little traffic with visions or the visionary.

He was fond of the old story about the man in the field who saw the writing in the sky, "G. P." and thought it meant "Go! Preach!" After a miserably unsuccessful ministry he found that the message was really "Go! Plough!" So much for visions, Father would say, and then he would press on to tend his sheep. So I certainly didn't bother him about Grandmother and God.

We were involved with the Church always. Father met Mother when he was rector of St. Peter's in Columbia, where Granddaddy was senior warden. Later we moved to New Orleans, where Father was rector of Trinity, and then he was called to St. Andrew's, Jackson, where he spent the rest of his ministry. Despite their differences in churchmanship Father and Grandmother were great friends. Grandmother often reminded us that we had the best father in the world. We did not question this, and we also thought we had the best grandmother. So as a courtesy to both of them I would be Low all winter with Father and High all summer with Grandmother, and we got along just fine until we began to argue about Mr. Norman.

We called him Mr. Norman but Grandmother called him Father Norman and that is what he called himself. He was an Anglo-Catholic priest who was trying to establish a religious community of some sort near Columbia, and having a tough go of it. His work was never clearly defined in my mind, but he called on Grandmother constantly for help and he always stayed for dinner. He had no sense of humor and he was not good with children, but he did wear interesting clothes and ornaments. Father's attitude toward Mr. Norman was uncharitable, to say the least, and this got on Grandmother's nerves. Father teased her about Mr. Norman, and wondered how he could keep his mind on the Lord when he was so busy changing his clothes in the chancel. Mr. Norman had services at St. Peter's occasionally when the rector was out of town, and he did put on quite a show. Grandmother was fascinated by him, and he couldn't change his clothes too often to suit her. He brought Grandmother books of devotions and Anglo-Catholic literature, and she added these to our daily Bible sessions. She learned a good deal that was not in the Prayer Book and she taught a lot of it to me. She set me to memorizing the Three Theological Virtues, the Four Cardinal Virtues, and Seven Gifts of the Holy

Spirit, and a good deal more, in mathematical progression.

I was delighted with the Seven Stages of Sin, and I was very pleased with a Form of Confession, but I hadn't been confirmed yet and I wasn't quite ready to think of Holy Communion as the Mass. Father complained a good deal about Mr. Norman, who was always around the house, and pointed out to Grandmother that he didn't seem to work at all. They got a little tense about Mr. Norman, but Grandmother didn't get too mad at Father because she really loved him very much, and then he fussed about Mr. Norman in a joking way and she would have to laugh. Grandmother and Father made it through August, and then Mr. Norman, being a little ahead of his time in this part of the country, went on off in search of the Liturgical Revival.

After Mr. Norman's departure there was nothing to argue about, and our summer routine continued until September. Nights were especially nice when everybody was home. That is, everybody but Walter, who was never home. On an August night we would finish supper and Grandmother and Granddaddy, Mother and Father and I would go out on the front porch and talk and watch the cars go by. The road in front of the house was not paved, but it was being surveyed for paving. The cars left plumes of dust behind them, and their headlights were pale yellow in the dust. The grown people would comment on the increase in automobile traffic on the Mt. Pleasant Pike in the last few years. Granddaddy and Father would light their El Roi Tan cigars, which were not permitted inside. The smoke from their cigars would drift slowly in the summer night, and when they drew on their cigars the ends glowed redly. They talked about when they were boys, the ladies talked about when they were girls, or about people they knew in Columbia or Nashville, and often a car would crunch up the drive and company would come in. Once the company told a thrilling tale about a prominent married man in Nashville who was in a wreck with some woman, not his wife. His wife threatened to shoot them both. I don't believe she shot anyone, but this was exciting word from the outside world, and the chairs rocked faster as the story was told. One night Grandmother and Granddaddy told about the dances they used to go to, and then they got up and did a polka by the light of the moon. Anyway, the cigars would glow, the rocking chairs would creak, lightning bugs would venture up on the porch and wink, a mourning dove would call from the fence, and sometimes the old owl in the dead tree in the Grants' yard would hoot. Much as I wanted to chase the lightning bugs, I would not leave the talk. The laughter was pleasant to hear, and usually somebody would ask Father to tell a story.

One of his favorites was about Willie May Loflin and her baptism. When Father was rector of St. Peter's in Columbia, a lady called on him to ask a special favor. She wanted to come into the Episcopal Church, and she had not been baptized. She believed that the only valid baptism was by immersion. She wanted to be baptized, she wanted her three children to be baptized, and she would like for Father to do the job. But she wouldn't feel right if she wasn't immersed. She firmly believed that only thus could she be sure of the authenticity of her regeneration, according to Scripture.

Father was very broad-minded about everything but Anglo-Catholics, and he thought that if Mrs. Loflin would feel better about being immersed, he would try to accommodate her. Immersion is permissible in the Episcopal Church, though affusion or sprinkling has long been the custom.

Father went to his friend Mr. Legion, the Baptist preacher, and asked to borrow his baptismal pool. Mr. Legion, a hearty fat man, agreed, and said he would be glad to lend Father his rubber undersuit. Father was tall and at the time slim, and there was a good deal of difference in his girth and in Mr. Legion's girth. The appointed day came, and Father, his convert, her husband, who was uneasy about the whole thing, and the three children presented themselves at the pool in the First Baptist Church. Father had on his vestments over Mr. Legion's baptizing suit. He began to read the Ministration of Holy Baptism, and got along fine with it until he got to the part having to do with water. Mrs. Loflin had renounced the devil and all his works, the vain pomp and glory of the world, and had promised to obediently keep God's holy will and commandments all the days of her life, when they got to the place in the service where Father asked the witnesses the name. Mr. Loflin named his wife Willie May, which had been her name all the time, Father took her by the hand, and the two of them processed into the pool, where Father was, according to the rubric, to "dip her in the Water discreetly."

When Father entered the pool the extra space in Mr. Legion's pants began to fill with air. Father grasped Willie May more firmly by the hand, and pressed on into deeper waters. The airy suit, now buoyant, floated upward, and Father floated with it. He lost his footing. He lost Willie May at the same time. Panic seized them both. Discretion was out of the question. The issue was survival, regenerate or not. When Father fought to get his feet on the bottom of the pool, the inflated rubber suit bore him up like water wings. He lunged toward Willie May, got her by the neck, and gasping for breath forced her head under, sputtering, "Willie May, I baptize thee in the name of the Father and the Son, and the Holy Ghost." By this time Mr. Loflin was about to come in after them, Mrs. Loflin had gotten over any reservations about the validity of sprinkling, and Father had nearly drowned. He and Mrs. Loflin bobbed to the surface, and worked their way to the edge of the pool, coughing and choking. As they reached shallow water and Father got a firm footing, Mrs. Loflin, her hair and eyes streaming, and fear written all over her face, gasped: "Mr. Capers, I want you to sprinkle the children!"

This always brought the house down of a summer evening long ago. Grandmother laughed until she cried. Soon it was time for bed. If the stars were out, Grandmother and I would go out in the yard for a last look at the night. "The heavens declare the glory of

God," said Grandmother, "and the earth sheweth his handiwork." The next day I would read and ride and say my memory work, High or Low. In the afternoon I could play in the tree house or bury treasures in a Whitman's candy box. There would be long conversations and tall tales on the porch at night. We would pray for Walter to get safely home from Nashville. September was in the air. Vacation time would soon be over. When we left, Moses took us to the C.M.A. station in the old Essex. Grandmother was on the porch, waving and crying.

Pass the Pesticide, Pappy

Pass the Pesticide, Pappy

Pass the Pesticide, Pappy

LONG AGO WHEN we were growing up in a big old house we knew that rats and mice were real and earnest, that mosquitoes bite, and that moth and rust doth corrupt. We dealt with these pests with the resources at hand. Traps and poison were available to our side.

The traps were baited and set by Father, who ducked no duties. Sometimes we would hear the traps go off, at which point the ladies would scream and hop up on a chair, and Father would dispatch the intruder. For moths, there were mothballs and frequent airings and sunnings, and for mosquitoes there were nets, and, later, sprays. Roaches were pretty unmentionable, but we knew that they marched about the kitchen at night, and we fed them a diet of roach paste on raw potato slices. In those days the termites were probably whittling away at us, but we didn't know it, and we pulled through the pests of our childhood to arrive fully grown in the brave new world of Pest Control.

All of us lucky home owners can now turn our problems over to professional exterminators. This is neater by far, though costlier, than the old way. We have one policy which protects us from roaches and rats, another for termites, and absolutely nothing for bees. This was brought to our attention during a recent crisis, when our yard man reported that he had been, in his own word, stang. Further, he said he would not be back until we got rid of the bumblebees nesting in the eaves of our homestead. We asked him if he would get rid of the bumblebees, but he said no, this is a job for specialists. So saying, he heaved his lawn mower into his pickup truck and roared away, leaving the grass with an abandoned look.

We called the pest control company with which we have two policies, only to find that bees, like fire ants, aren't included. The gentleman to whom we spoke explained that bee work is highly specialized, just like the yard man said, and therefore, extry. We said, go ahead, we must get the yard cut, and we don't care to be stang by a bumblebee anyway.

This is how we found out a few fairly interesting facts about bees. We found that five o'clock in the afternoon is Bee Time, when the bees come home after a hard day of stanging. Therefore, five o'clock is the best time to exterminate them, as well as any guests you may have in the house who do not know it is Bee Time. In our own particular case, two Bee Men came to exterminate our bees with a very heady gas. At the same time we had two adult and three children guests. The gas got to the guests, who coughed and choked a bit, but not to the bees, who came in as usual the next afternoon at Bee Time.

We reported this failure to the pest control company specialist, who admitted that he had not only underestimated our bees, he had misjudged them. He thought they were carpenter bees, who only chew down your house, but they turned out to be bumblebees, just like the yard man said. And true to their nature, they had stang his exterminators.

"Bumblebees is extry," he said, "I made you a price on carpenter bees, but bumblebees is extry."

About this time we were getting more information about bees than we were really interested in, but we agreed to his terms so that we could get on with our daily duties and qualify to have the grass cut.

It so happened that while the bumblebee squad was going up and down a ladder at the side of our house, the regular contract pest squad came to perform a routine check-up on our rat, mouse and roach population. This is when we got the telephone call from our below-stairs tenant, who had noticed the army of exterminators. She wanted to show us something. As she has been known to complain mildly about creeping, crawling things, we responded to her call with apprehension. We were amazed to find her leaning fondly over a glass cage which contained two rats.

"I wanted you to see the gerbils," she said, "I want to be sure the pest control people don't hurt them."

"Those are rats," I said, "and I pay a lot of money to have them controlled."

"On the contrary, these are gerbils," she said, "and I paid a lot of money for them because they are said to be wonderful pets."

Plainly, this is a problem. Pets or pests? Pests or pets? The dictionary, where we seek solace when human aid fails, bears us out. A gerbil is "a burrowing leaping desert rodent," and if that isn't a rat I'll eat my hat. No, the way things are going the gerbil will probably eat it. And shortly thereafter, if our luck holds, the carpenter bees will hammer, the bumblebees will stang, and the mailman will deliver a frightening note from the pest control people, to the effect that gerbil control isn't included, but they did it anyway.

Ivy League

THE MOST FASCINATING mail we get is addressed "Occupant." Recently we received an especially helpful lawn and garden guide. On page eight of the guide we are advised to "think like a rose." Further investigation reveals that a thinking rose would have a lot to worry about. There are aphids, which feed on rose sap, thrips which attack it in summer, mites, black spot, rust and mildew.

It is hard enough to think like a person, but if you add the worries of a rose to income tax payments, the vagaries of the stock market, Viet Nam, situation morality, the sex revolution, and cosmetics for men, you might as well let the thrips have at you.

Another piece in the guide is entitled "My Greatest Moment in Gardening." Ours came today, when, seeking inspiration, we looked out into our own front yard. Lifting our eyes, we beheld a beer can imprisoned in the top of our wisteria vine. How the beer can got there we do not know, but it was a pretty great moment in gardening. We could imagine passers-by saying either, "That lady is a real nut," or "That lady is an old soak." We attacked the offender with a golf club, and thereupon adopted our garden policy for the year.

If you cannot garden yourself, choose neighbors who can. This is equally inspiring and less exhausting. From April to early June we live in a bower of bloom. Azaleas and camellias next door, iris and roses across the street, and as the seasons change, golden daylilies and gaudy zinnias everywhere.

Our own gardening history is bad. We have tried all the vainly so-called "fool-proof, you-can't-kill-it, it-will-grow-anywhere" plants. But they are not fool-proof against us, we can kill it, and it will grow nowhere, once we have touched it with our far from green thumb. We tried petunias last year, and bought a good deal of delicious plant food for their little beds. They held their heads high in the sunset. In the dawning, they were gone. "Slugs," said gardeners wisely. "Snails." We have tried bulbs. Our first and last flower this spring was a King Alfred jonquil. One. The King. Alfred was dandy, but lonely, and when his life span was over, our garden ceased to grow.

So now we accept the fact that we cannot garden. We regard all gardeners with awe. When day is done, we retire to our boudoir to admire the only green growing thing we have not been able to kill. This is a sturdy stand of ivy which grows right through our window frame. It not only grows, it thrives. We have been told that we should cut it, that it looks peculiar, and that it may reach over and strangle us in the night.

The peril is negligible compared to the pleasure of sharing a room with something so dauntless. The ivy has become our green badge of courage. If the ivy can make it without Tender Loving Care, then maybe so can we! Thrips may come and thrips may go, but so long as the ivy pushes through the bedroom wall, we face the future unafraid!

My Dog Holly

THIS IS A LITTLE piece about my dog Holly, but it isn't going to end "If I should hang from the highest hill, I know whose love would follow me still," et cetera, et cetera. Because if I should hang from the highest hill, I know Holly's love would follow the nearest can of all-meat dog food. We watch television together, and she has refused to have anything to do with cereal dog foods since she saw the Alpo commercial. Determination is the key to Holly's character.

I got Holly one Christmas, and named her for the season and because she hollered all night. This was a poor joke at the time, and hasn't gotten much funnier since Holly grew to be known as the Terrible Terrier of St. Ann Street. I didn't choose Holly, she chose me. This is sappy, but true. I went to the pet shop with no idea of getting a pet. This is more understandable when I tell you that it was really a garden shop, with a few pets thrown in. I went for fertilizer, and came out with a female puppy. When I looked at the two puppies left in the dismal chicken-wire pen, Holly reached out a paw and grabbed me. She did not weep or moan, and she surely did not cringe. She just perked up her ears, held her tail high, and grabbed me. Then she slapped me on the wrist with her paw, as if to say, "Here! Take me! Let's get the hell out of here!" I think Holly would have said hell instead of heck, for she is very tough.

Now she is ten years old and weighs twenty pounds, and is not afraid of the devil, large dogs, or the laundry-man. I can't speak for the devil and large dogs, but the laundryman is afraid of her. And well he might be, for her consuming ambition is to eat him alive.

When Holly first saw a swimming pool, she jumped in. When she went riding for the first time she jumped out the window. When anyone comes to call, she jumps on the caller. In other words, Holly is a jumper.

I am making these notes on Holly because she lives dangerously, and I am reminded of the impermanence of life by the way she hurtles through it. She has just attacked a very large furry black dog, and is sitting at my feet with one bloody ear, spitting out black fur. I can tell by her complacent expression that she thinks she won the fight, though such is not the case. One can never tell when she will land in jail or the hospital, so I had better immortalize her while I can.

After one of Holly's altercations I took her to the vet for repairs, and asked him what he thought about her future. He said that one female dog, especially a wire, will always fight another female dog, and that women just plain don't like one another. I don't think this is entirely true, but Holly certainly subscribes to the theory. With these facts in hand, I have done what I can to protect the neighbors. I have no patience with so-called animal lovers who let their animals disturb people and property, so I built a fence. It is a maximum security fence, and quite expensive.

The fence goes down below ground level, and is lined with chicken wire, for terriers are diggers. It goes up above the ground and turns back over the yard, with more chicken wire, for terriers are jumpers. And here I kept her very well, most of the time. But in icy wet weather it was a chore for me to go out and feed her, so I had to figure a way to get her into the house. I designed a secret passageway from her yard through the basement and then up a sort of jungle gym to the floor of the kitchen, where a trap door gives access to the house. If Holly were not an athlete, she couldn't make it. An incredulous carpenter carried out the design, in an embarrassed manner, and now Holly pops up on call. Late one night a gentleman caller brought me home from a party and asked about Holly. In reply, Holly popped up through the kitchen floor. "My God!"

screamed the caller, as Holly materialized and jumped on him. My rule is that Holly stays in her yard or pops up into the house, though I must say that on occasion and with the use of her teeth she has managed to climb out of the yard.

I thought perhaps motherhood would gentle Holly. So I arranged an alliance with the Judge, an elderly registered wire with an enviable stud record. Holly and the Judge had a brief but meaningful relationship, and I did everything just right for the mother-to-be. The vet, a visionary type, told me to build her a little nest in the basement and line it with old newspapers. According to his vision, one day I would find a new little family there. I doubted that, for Holly has her own very firm ideas about everything, and there was no reason to think that motherhood would be an exception. It certainly was not. When her time was upon her, Holly swung up through the jungle gym into the kitchen, and waddled toward the over-stuffed chair in the living room. There was no stopping her. She went to the chair like a martin to his gourd. She settled into the chair, and produced eight puppies before the startled gaze of a lady caller who had brought my mother some soup. Holly labored on, the soup hit the ceiling, and the lady caller was never seen again. The point of this story is that motherhood did not gentle Holly.

When Holly is crossed, which is seldom, she becomes very agitated. I do cross her whenever I have company, for I am of the vanishing school that believes guests should not be physically assaulted by dogs or children. So when company comes, I put Holly out or shut her up in a little broom closet at the foot of the attic steps. One day I put her in the broom closet, and she tore on up the attic steps, only to crash through the attic-fan opening and fall eleven feet to the floor below. There was a sickening thump, and I dreaded the sight I knew I would find—Holly all broken and bloody, in a heap on the floor. Not at all. She got up, shook herself, gasped for breath, said "Uh!" and jumped on the guest.

When I think Holly is improving, she has a relapse. The first year of her life she ate several hand-knit sweaters and a very nice coat. When we would rush for the stomach pump, the vet would find an amazing collection of rocks, glass, nails, wool yarn, and "footlets," the little foot socks I wear in the summertime. None of this disturbed Holly's digestion, so I cut out the pumping, and her diet eventually became more conventional. But she found other outlets. I cannot forget the gentleman caller who offered to take her out for a stroll on her leash. As he stood on the curb holding the leash, and chatting with me, Holly lost patience and lunged into the street. The next thing I knew the gentleman caller was in a heap in the middle of the street, his new pants torn, and his wallet and keys scattered about him. Holly, ears alert and tongue lolling, was watching him critically and waiting for him to get up and finish what he had begun, her walk.

As Holly gets older, in common with all of us, she develops little quirks. Now she clacks her teeth together in a regular rhythm, like an old woman with an ill-fit plate. When she wants something done, she wants it right now, and to emphasize this she jumps up in my lap, fixes me with a glittering eye, and clacks her plate in my face. This is her nearest approach to affection. As a matter of fact, Holly is not affectionate, and my company quickly bores her unless our television program concerns animals or food.

Beulah, who is my friend and servant and who has been with me since I was five years old, loves Holly, and is very good to her. It bothers Beulah that Holly does not seem to reciprocate. Sometimes Beulah complains, "Holly didn't say anything to me this morning." Sure enough, she doesn't say much. The only time I think she cares for me is when I take a trip. She watches my packing preparations disdainfully, saying nothing, and sniffing a little scornfully. But when I come back she races around her pen ninety miles an hour, clacking her plate in joyful welcome, and even whimpering a little in a display of emotion which must embarrass her.

So, if I should hang from the highest hill, or just plain die in my bed, I don't think Holly would care too much, if she continued to get her all-meat dog food. But she is my companion, and I don't mind saying that I'm very fond of her. After all, she has a good many virtues, if I can think of them. She's determined, and that can be a virtue. She's brave, as the harassed laundryman would be the first to agree. She certainly wouldn't burn her draft card, if there was a chance of a fight ahead. So I guess we could say that Holly's got *heart*. But if Beulah or Dr. Dolittle could get Holly to speak, I'm afraid she'd put it, "I've got *guts*, you mean, and *damn* that laundryman!"

Moving Day

NEXT TO A WAR, which shouldn't necessarily happen in each generation, there is nothing so soul-shaking as a move, which generally comes once in a lifetime to all men. This reporter, recently packed in paper shavings, bundled up in a large moving van, and transported from scenes of childhood to new environs, has some advice, won the hard way, for all movers. As it is presumed that everyone is a mover, a potential mover or a past mover, perhaps the perils of the shared experience will fall on eager ears.

First, don't try to pack your clothes on M day. Wear them all. You may startle your new neighbors if you arrive in August wearing an old mink, but you will startle them more if you appear the next day wearing nothing at all, because you can't find anything. Then, if your move is still in the future, avoid the collection of possessions. Family portraits are a definite drag, as the gilt is sure to be knocked off Uncle Charlie if you move any distance at all. We have even known some ancestral eyes to be punched out, and by the most reliable moving companies.

You should especially beware the acquiring and reading of books. Cultivate a vacant mind. If read you must, go to the public library. For if you have lived for years with Miss Minerva and William Green Hill, Jo March, Becky Sharp and Leora Arrowsmith, or even with Scarlett O'Hara and Amber and Lady Chatterley, you will find it impossible to part with them, and they cost a pretty penny per hour to move, just like the old rocking chair or the kitchen stove.

As your household furnishings and appliances fall apart, discard them. March them straight out to the garbage department, and leave them with never a backward glance. If you don't, the day will surely come when you can't even give them away, and they must be hauled to the new locale. Here they will almost inevitably land on some narrow stair, which you will fall up or down the rest of your life.

About family photographs. Those fading brown snapshots of Aunt Emma and little Davey by the old place in the country might as well go too. They couldn't possibly interest anyone but Aunt Emma and little Davey, and by the time you move chances are Aunt Emma has gone to glory and little Davey has married a city wife, who doesn't have room for the family album in her apartment.

Finally, about memories. Those old letters tied with blue might as well go in the incinerator right now. Harden your heart, light a match, and watch them go, in a curl of smoke. When you get ready to move, they will not only break your heart, they will break you, period. For there is a price on memories and it comes high. It's the same old hourly rate, and a memory is worth infinitely more than that, or nothing at all.

Wreck

AS I WAS HIT by a truck on deadline day it was inevitable that I should write about my wreck. I am shaken, quaken, shattered and battered, but grateful I was able to walk away. My Buick Special was not so fortunate, and had to be towed away as a result of its encounter with a pickup truck from Lee County, Mississippi, on a peaceful Sunday morning in the spring. The truck was apparently lost in space after a Sunday drive on the interstate highways, and was trying to find the Baptist Hospital to visit relatives. Anyway, it turned up in my neighborhood, ran a stop sign, and ploughed into me as I was driving quietly to church, accompanied by my nine-year-old godchild and namesake, who was just up from an appendectomy.

I hope you will note that we have all the elements of a soap opera here, and we almost had one. The truck crashed into the left side of my car, the driver's side, with a tremendous bang. When I recovered my senses enough to look about me, I saw that the neighborhood had gathered, in various stages of Sunday dress and undress, to admire the wreck. We soon had a cloud of witnesses which included four dogs, who immediately began to fight underneath the truck.

The driver of the truck was a gentleman without any teeth, and my first thought was that he had knocked them out on us. Charlotte was screaming, "Oh, my back!" I was thinking about her front, recently sewed up after the appendectomy, and my own reaction was a general palsied trembling which reduced me to a jelly and left me unable to speak without a quaver.

"Call the police," I quavered, after kind passersby had stopped and carried Charlotte off to the house of a long-suffering neighbor who lives on the corner where the wreck occurred, and consequently does a lot of first aid work, as it is a bad corner.

I wanted to lie right down in the middle of the street, but felt that I should stick with the car until the law arrived. More neighbors appeared, some in jump suits, some in sweat shirts and shorts, some in slacks, and a good many in coats, ties, dresses and hats, as we were blocking a vital artery which feeds into the downtown churches. Even in shock, I was reminded of the night we had a fire in the neighborhood. We all rushed out of our houses to see what was going on. For days we discussed what everybody slept in. The wreck provided a parallel social note on Sunday morning life styles in southern suburbia.

The gathering was friendly, helpful, and concerned, except for the dogs, who continued to fight beneath the truck. An old cocker spaniel, agitated by our big bang, leapt at the throat of a mournful Weimaraner, and two terriers, impelled by their very nature, joined the fray. No one ran away from the scene of the crash, many stepped forward to volunteer as witnesses, and we had several offers of rides to the emergency room. All in all, it was an exceptionally friendly southern-type wreck. My assailant and I, addled by the crash, shook hands for lack of anything better to do, though he still remained toothless and silent. I noticed his lady companions in the cab of the truck, and they were his female counterparts. Neither lady had teeth; they were weathered and worn and appeared to be completely resigned, as if the Lord had laid His hand upon them and decreed that they should strike an Episcopalian at the intersection of Poplar and Greymont on a Sunday morning, and if so, amen. Naturally, they had no liability insurance.

When the police arrived I found my voice, and while the police were polite, one of them did say, "Lady, please let us finish." What they had to finish was asking questions, and at this point our volunteer witness stepped forward and turned out to have the most wonderful qualifications for her role.

"Name," the police officer said. "Occupation."

"I teach driver education," she said firmly, "and I saw it all happen."

I still had to call Charlotte's mother and inform her that in my efforts to get my godchild to Sunday worship I had almost finished her off. Charlotte, meantime, in the neighborly emergency room, was conducting herself beautifully, but when I appeared she burst forth afresh in stentorian sobs. My voice went into quaver, and I don't know how Charlotte's mother got the message, but she did, and soon appeared to take Charlotte off for a checkup. In passing she mentioned that she never saw so many hats at a wreck.

Well, that's about it. It's true what the safety people say about accidents happening close to home. We were a block and a half from home when struck. Also, buckle up. I had on my seat belt, Charlotte did not. You can't be too careful, for some poor soul, confused by the proliferation of highway signs like "Do Not Enter," "Wrong Way," "Exit Coming," and then "Exit Gone," may just give up, spin off, and sock it to you. I think some of the evangelical signs from country roads should be transferred to city streets, like "Prepare to Meet Your God." Keep your insurance paid up, and have frequent medical examinations to see if you are blind or crazy. If you have a child in the car, double your precautions and insist that he fasten his seat belt.

I don't know what happened to my assailant, poor fellow. He was unhurt and unruffled, but plainly delayed and perhaps had to spend the night in Jackson. Charlotte got to wear a sling to school for a couple of days. Friendly neighbors took me off for a Sunday morning refreshment to calm my nerves. Leaving the scene of the crash I glanced at the Buick. Like Judge Moody's hapless Buick in Eudora Welty's wonderfully funny book, *Losing Battles*, it looked "like a booger had a fit in it."

Not Speaking of Operations

SINCE MY EXPERIENCE with surgery, it has been suggested by friends calling on the sick that I write a piece about my operation. The implication is that such a piece would be a howl. Certainly they always have been! My answer to such suggestions, graciously intended, is a categorical "No!"

In the first place, I found nothing funny—I can easily refrain from saying side-splitting—about the removal of my gall bladder. This is a revolting allusion, but if President Johnson can mention his, I can mention mine. As the job was done with skill and as I was treated kindly, I have nothing of special interest to report. I do not remember the operation, thankfully, but one of my friends reports that I never looked better than I did when I came from the Recovery Room. This is a hard way to look good, and I will probably never look that good again, so we might as well settle for my conscious worried expression.

I am told that I behaved satisfactorily, did nothing untoward in the operating room, and "came to" murmuring politely, "Oh, mercy!" You can't beat that for decorum. The first meal that was placed before me, or upon me, to be exact, consisted of fried catfish and cornbread. I still think this must have been meant for the patient next door, but maybe not, for I ate it and got along with it just fine.

In the second place, about not writing the funny piece, any minor inconveniences or frustrations incident to a hospital stay are not worth mentioning, as who knows, I might have to go back!

I do have a good deal to say about, and for, convalescence. There was one bad night when I came home, and those dearer to me than near had provided what is known in nursing circles as a Sitter to sit with me. The Sitter was very nice, but she walked around the house all night, went to the bathroom a good deal, and got up at four-thirty to make coffee. I crawled out to have coffee with her in the living room so she wouldn't come in to have coffee with me in the bedroom, and from four-thirty to six a.m. she regaled me with tales of her former patients, all, as she put it, "a little mindless." By six o'clock I was about to join their group, so I wrote her a check in a trembling hand, thanked her for her trouble, and sent her on her way. Since then everything has been fine. Beulah volunteered to take the afternoon shift, and Holly, the Courageous Wire-Haired Terrier, defends me at night. Knowing full well that I risk comparison with one of the more offensive literary creations of all time, Pollyanna the Glad Girl, if I say It Was All For the Best, I will now take that risk.

While the Giant Gallstone doesn't stand up prettily beside the shells of Sanibel Island, where Anne Morrow Lindbergh found her Gift from the Sea, the effect was about the same. For the first time in my life I have stayed away from work without a feeling of guilt. I was *ordered* to stay in, and that was that. So I relaxed and enjoyed it.

Spring is wonderful anywhere—on Sanibel Island, in the Rockies, on the olive slopes of Italy, in any countryside, in my own front yard. I had time to check up on all the others that live here with me, truly enough, the birds and the bees. I didn't spot any fine birds that have to be lured to the window sill by fancy diets, but the plain marauders after hedge berries and grass seed are surely worth knowing. Handsome bluejays, iridescent grackles, testy mockingbirds whose sweet song belies their black hearts, and the common little sparrows that live in the louvers of my attic think this is their home, and so do the squirrels that eat up all the pecans, and an almost tame rabbit that comes up from the Pearl River swamp early in the morning and lopes around the yard. The mockingbirds must have been the first settlers here, for they have a proprietary air. They dive at interlopers walking under their watch tower on the eaves, including me. And only the mockingbirds can intimidate Holly the Courageous Wire-Haired Terrier. While I was still at home the redbirds began to come, and this was quite a show, all acted out under a sky as blue as the Aegean Sea.

The bees are here too, swarming around some sweet flowering bush that must surely be a volunteer, as I never pause to plant in my normal hurried routine. So, the sun shines, the sky is blue, the bees are after the honey, and the birds and squirrels make about as much sense with their chatter as a lot of people running around in circles trying to do too many things they think they have to do.

Which brings me to the bittersweet realization that my office functions just fine without me. This is a tribute to the people with whom I work, and it is also a load off my mind. You see, as I become more unloaded and more mindless, I unwind more, my batteries begin to re-charge, and I contemplate only occasionally the necessity of working for a living.

Another bonus of convalescence, or changing pace. Books. I was sent or lent Peanuts and Pogo, *The Boston Strangler* and *Madame Sarah, The Christian Agnostic* and *Playboy* magazine, Art Buchwald and Elia Kazan, Mary Renault's Greek novels and *The Secret of Santa Vittoria,* and a lot more besides, since the Giant Gallstone stopped me in my tracks. I used to read for sheer pleasure. In my job, I have to read for information. And in my time, I have reviewed a good many books for a small fee. It has been years and years since I could pile up five or six or ten books and just read because I wanted to, no deadlines, no criticisms to weigh carefully, just entertainment, and if it isn't, I can surely put the book down. I may say that a lot that is written now isn't entertainment, but then you say, if you're so smart, why aren't you rich?

Finally, People. People like friends who Rally Round, Turn Up and Stand By. People like my tenants, who for the first time in our lessor-lessee relationship rushed in with the rent check on the first of the month and refrained from mentioning any part of my house that had fallen or leaked on them during my illness. People like neighbors I don't ordinarily see, like old friends I haven't seen in a long time. People who write notes and send cards to let you know that they are concerned about you. This is worth knowing, and let this be a lesson to all of us who don't write notes or send cards. People like Beulah. But then there aren't any more people like Beulah, who stayed five extra hours every day for two weeks for friendship and not for pay, which she didn't want to take.

So now if you think that I am suggesting that you all line up and have your gall bladder out, you're wrong. I am suggesting that a break in routine, voluntary or enforced, can be helpful. The car pool driver, the maker of beds and cooker of dinners, the club woman and the woman who works, can all use a quiet time. Maybe you can manage to stop, to slow down, to evaluate, to appreciate, without an experience with the internist, the radiologist, the anesthesiologist, the surgeon, the nurses, the hospital, and the bank. But if you can't, take it from one who was forced out of the Big Push temporarily. Stop in your tracks. Sniff the wind. Look up at the sky. Let go. Turn loose. If you can go away and lie in the sun by the sea, by all means do so. But if you can't, perhaps you could change the lead on your canter in the same old ring! It would be worth a great deal to you if you could, because we all have what Will Percy described as "a need of silence and of stars," and we surely have to fight for it. This is worth fighting for, and I couldn't have done it myself without the Giant Gallstone. Talk, talk, talk, is about my speed. But if I *can* practice what I preach, friends, then indeed the Giant Gallstone will turn out to have been a Pearl of Great Price. We shall see!

The Pain of It All

The Pain of It All

WHEN ONE OF MY BEST friends left the hospital during my operation before she heard whether I had lived or died, so she could get home in time to see her noontime television program, I realized the grip that soap operas have on the ladies of our land. Of course I did not realize it at the time, as I was unconscious. A couple of years later an eyewitness told me about it. Then I wondered what the soap operas have that I haven't got. After a week of viewing, I am thankful to say, plenty.

The week of viewing was brought on by my belated purchase of a tiny color telly. It is so tiny that I have to view it on my lap, and then I squint and cry because of the orange and green people so close to me. Even so, I can tell that everyone on the screen is in bad trouble. If there is anyone in the world who has not seen a couple of hours of soap opera, let me tell you what to expect.

First, there is very dismal music, like a violin crying. Then a character appears, usually in a white coat to indicate that he is a doctor. He sighs heavily. Next, a female character appears, and she sighs heavily. It is not immediately apparent to the irregular viewer what they are sighing about, but you soon get the idea that things are bad and likely to get worse. And so they do. My first sampling turned up a sighing man who had been lost ever since World War II. He wants to divorce his wife. She has chest pains. The first time around I didn't know who was in the right, the lost man or the lady with chest pains. They both sigh gustily. Then their little girl appears. She loves them both, and she sighs a lot too. Next, we meet a father, a brother, and innumerable other relatives, all worried to death. The time between commercials is devoted to family discussions about why the lost man wants to divorce his wife. The brother, who is going blind, thinks that being lost so long may have affected his virility. What he doesn't know is, the lady with chest pains was frequently unfaithful during her husband's absence, and has been corespondent in several divorce cases. The family apparently didn't miss her while she was in court. Anyway, they think she is lovely. The little girl breaks down and weeps, and a tiny tot appears, and tells her she is like a flower which has ceased to bloom.

At this point I went blind too, right along with the brother, but for different reasons. His case was never diagnosed, but mine was caused by proximity to the tiny tube and all that living color. Anyway, I missed the point, if there was one, while I wept briefly. The next thing I saw was a lady in a hospital bed with a tube in her nose. I noticed in one day's viewing three principal characters with tubes in their noses. This lady is unconscious, but she is able to sigh heavily. A bunch of doctors come in, all kin to principal characters, and they sigh too. It seems that the lady's illegitimate son, who is a doctor, has operated on her by mistake, and another doctor just told him what he has done. This shakes him up and his breathing is affected, while various nurses, all kin to principal characters, try to convince him that his mother really loves him, though she gave him away when he was born.

This drama fades out to the sobbing of violins, or maybe cellos, and the next program opens in Operating Room 28. There is a lady screaming on the table with a Band-Aid on her head, and a bunch of doctors lean over her, sighing heavily. The lady continues to scream, and one particularly nervous doctor pounds his head with his fist. The scene shifts from Operating Room 28 to a private hospital room, where a man I couldn't place was going blind. I don't think this was the same blind man we had before, as it was a different program, but he was just as mixed up as the first one. He doesn't know how to tell his wife that he divorced her while she was on a shopping trip, and I do think that would be hard to explain. He has a teen-age son whose mother is not the wife who went on the shopping trip, and here the plot eluded me completely.

The next scene opens in another hospital room, and herein lies a gentleman with a heart condition who is quoting Shakespeare. His girl friend leans over him worriedly, and he murmurs, "Parting is such sweet sorrow." The lady is still screaming in Operating Room 28, but the nervous doctor has come out, torn off his surgical mask, dashed down a drink of water from the water cooler, and put his head in his hands. We leave him thus downcast, and without a word of warning we are shifted into the kitchen of another doctor, whose daughter has left her bridegroom at the altar because she is afraid she can't handle his children by his first wife, and because, you guessed it, *she* is going blind. This is a secret shared only by *her* doctor, and I don't know whose brother he is.

So this is how it goes, day in and day out on the tiny tube. Thousands look and listen, are moved, and leave old friends unconscious to see how it all comes out. Three weeks or three years later that same poor lady may be screaming in Operating Room 28. But the formula is a great success, as any wise soap seller will tell you, and a lot of ladies and some gentlemen take their phones off the hooks from twelve to three each working day, so they can keep up with the pain of it all.

The first two programs I watched were sponsored by Joy and Cheer.

Be It Ever So

THERE IS A GOOD deal to be said for the comforts of home as opposed to the lure of faraway places. No matter how fancy the fare, there is something about your own personal bath and your own personal bed that can't be beat on the European plan.

We have a friend who goes alone to Riverside Park from time to time, cheese sandwich in hand. There she sits, nibbles the sandwich, and contemplates. Whether she contemplates the infinite, the swimming pool, the tennis court, or the sheer joy of being away from work, we know not, but we do know that she is a serene character, and that she recommends at least one lone luncheon a week at Riverside Park. This is noted for the benefit of the less ambitious wage slave, who just can't see fighting a tennis ball in the summer sun.

If you work for a living, chances are you haven't been to the zoo in quite a while. You might want to visit it. Some of its simian residents may call to mind forgotten friends, and there is a new lion's den, from which no Daniel could ever escape. We trust the same applies to the lions, who apparently roam at will among craggy paths that simulate their native habitat. The elephants are as heartwarming as ever. In fact, they appear to be the same elephants I knew as a child. This is probably untrue, but no one would know but another elephant. Elephants seem to have good dispositions and even better digestions, as they wear a pleasant expression and eat peanuts all day. Most of the animals seem to be affected by the heat and smell mighty bad, it is only fair to tell you, but they do take your mind off the office.

If you work an eight-hour day, you might like to go to an afternoon movie, just to prove that it can be done. If you drink beer or whisky, try a chocolate ice cream soda for a change, if you can find one. This is a very fine drink, and may have been neglected by some who strayed from dairy products long ago. Whatever you do, let it be different from the old routine. And next week, I will let you know the results of practicing what I preach, for I plan to take a few days' holiday at home.

* * * * *

Silly old me! Last week I wrote a cheerful little piece about how joyful it is to spend your vacation at home. I outlined a program of activities within the city limits, guaranteed to make you happy. To tell you the truth, I even believed it, when I wrote it.

If anyone else believed it, and on the strength of this made plans to spend a holiday at home, cancel at once. I have never had a more exhausting week, financially and physically. When I am at work, it doesn't worry me that the gutter leaks and the yard grows prize-winning hay. When I am at home, I am moved to fix everything, and the result is total disability.

My schedule worked fine, for a couple of days. Then I got all dressed up in golf clothes, and went around nine holes in weather fit only for mad dogs and Englishmen. For a lady who hasn't played more than three holes at a time in some years, this was wearing. I tottered back to the clubhouse seeing stars and stripes and hearing faint music.

After this slight setback I was afraid to venture forth among athletes. I stayed at home a while and this is when I got my fix-everything complex. The rains came, the grass grew, and the gutter leaked. I advanced on all of these problems, and the die was cast.

I met a lot of interesting people on my vacation. I saw

a great deal of the gutter man, the yard man, and an itinerant carpenter who somehow heard about me, and came by to remind me that my house was about to fall off its foundation.

I even saw the doctor, as this was fix-everything week. Although his comment was merely a cryptic "a watched pot never boils," I was well past the boiling point and well on my way to an explosion. About this time the insurance industry, en masse, called to tell me where I could put the money I had just put in the gutter, and the yard, and the doctor.

Now the week is over, and not a minute too soon. I must return to the office to fight the good fight. I had the gutter fixed, and this reminded the gutter man that the cornices are rotting. I somehow bought some St. Augustine sod, probably as a result of the slight set-back. I have no one to plant the sod, if that is what you do with it. If anyone should plant it, and grass should spring from it, I will have to employ someone to mow it. If no one mows it, I will watch it grow and cry, and think that I could have had a nice weekend at Point Clear for the price of it.

As I said, I am financially shattered as a result of my economical week at home. I have also developed insomnia, broken only by a recurring nightmare. In the nightmare I am riding a tractor around a field of alfalfa, upon which a broken gutter spews forth floods of rainwater. I wear a frantic expression, and in the dream I chant over and over, in a cracked voice, "Charge it."

So now my duty to my readers is clear. I must warn them. Let my vacation be a lesson to you! Get out of town! Tomorrow I will be back at work, and that right early. For be it ever so humble, there is no place like the office.

Queen of the May

"WAKE ME EARLY, Mother dear, for I'm to be the Queen of the May." Long ago in Merrie England whence many of our customs came, a young lass was chosen May Queen to reign over the spring festival in her parish. Years pass, oceans are crossed, and in the New World, tradition survives. The queen thing really caught on. When the Royal Barge floats down the Mississippi River bearing the rulers of the Memphis Cotton Carnival, you may be sure a queen will float thereon. And the carnivals and balls and festivals throughout the South celebrating social and religious traditions or great crops or industries, or both, all have their focus on a queen.

Our part of the country has always been crazy for queens, and Sir Walter Scott had a lot to do with this. The nineteenth century Mississippian who settled the Delta, for instance, read Scott avidly. He patterned his ring tournaments on the knightly games of the days of chivalry. Local knights rode wildly at rings with home-made lances, and the winner was rewarded for risking his neck by an accolade from the Queen of Love and Beauty. And now we have queens of pilgrimage, queens of balls, and queens of almost any crop that grows.

So far, so pretty, Queen of the May and Queen of Love and Beauty are tender titles. Queen of the Cotton Carnival has a majestic ring. Queen of the Apple Blossom Festival is a beautiful thought. The Cherry Blossom Queen sounds delectable. Just plain Queen of the Carnival Ball is pretty good. But the traditional queen ritual is about to get out of hand.

Pick up your local paper, and chances are you will read about the Pickle Queen, the Butterfat Queen or the Ham Queen. The Bean Queen and the Mule Queen are honorable if not euphonious titles. We have attended coronation ceremonies for the Shrimp Queen and the Broiler Queen, and we understand that the Yam Queen is highly regarded. There must be a Crawfish Queen and a Muskrat Queen in the Cajun country of Louisiana, and the possibility of a Sour Mash Queen in the hills of Tennessee is not beyond imagination.

These titles are created because some promoters of foods, goods and services have no ear for the cadences of language. They are engaged in a perfectly legitimate effort to sell their products or to celebrate a harvest, and to honor an attractive young girl in the process. This is all to the good, but too often the aesthetics of the affair seem to elude them.

The natural resources of our area suggest a multitude

of queens. Iris and azaleas, okra, grits and cheese, peanuts, tobacco and loblolly pine, strawberries, sugar cane and rice—you can pay your money and take your choice. But it is possible that some thoughtful future queen may hesitate to wear the proffered crown. The honor is as great with the grits as with the strawberries, to be sure, but the strawberries sound better. And while the sugar refining industry is no more respectable than the pork producing industry, who wants to be queen of the pigs?

Tell Me About Your Trip

SOME VERY YOUNG people make some very sage remarks. For example, we know a nine-year-old girl who has just returned from an exciting trip to New York. There she saw many sights, went to some Broadway plays, and rode the camels in the Bronx Zoo. "You'll have a lot to tell when you get home," said her aunt, who took her. "But I may never get to tell it," was the knowing reply.

This nine-year-old knew that people practically never listen to other people, because she is a very observant child. For all her nine years she must have noticed that

"Did you have a good trip?" is almost as rhetorical a question as "How do you feel?"

Just try to tell somebody about your trip. Try to tell somebody anything. It is generally a losing fight. We have known some very interesting people in our day, but we've never noticed anyone paying much attention to their eyewitness accounts of exciting persons, places or events.

One of our friends had the harrowing adventure of going down on the *Athenia*. Happily she came back up, and was thus able to tell the inside story of a dramatic event that influenced the course of history. Do you think anyone wanted to hear it? Why, no!

We introduced her proudly as a shipwreck survivor. "She went down on the *Athenia*," we said, thinking she would be interviewed immediately.

"Have a cracker," was the reaction, and then later, "Oh, the *Titanic*!"

So it goes, with variations, all along the line. Returning natives who have spent years in faraway places might as well pick up the thread of conversation where they left it off, and omit that funny (they thought) story about cocktails with the headhunters of Ubangi.

Because whether it's the *Athenia*, the camels at the Bronx Zoo or the Ubangi headhunters, the story doesn't have a chance when it runs into competition on the local level. The hit of the week still goes like this: "The maid was late, the bridge club was coming, and by the time we got to the grocery, all the fresh crabmeat was gone."

We will admit, of course, that there may be a valid reason behind the general unwillingness to listen. And it isn't all egocentricity. Back of it may be honest fear, based on sad experience. Once, years ago, you may have said in an unguarded moment: "Tell us about your trip." With which the eager traveler, like a thirsty wanderer finding an oasis in the desert, got the bit between his teeth and was good for several hours.

This can happen, and is to be avoided at all costs. Once in the spotlight, it is possible for a traveler to go on for indefinite periods of time, and still be only two days out on the *Queen Elizabeth*. And if he has returned from a two months' vacation, you can see the horrid potentialities. This is a far more awful fate than listening to a diary of domesticity, and yet it does seem a shame that our nine-year-old, sure enough, may never get to tell about the camels.

Good Sport

THE WORLD OF SPORT intrigues us. Lady athletes excite our admiration. When we began to grow, and continued to grow taller and taller, our parents said hopefully, "She will be a good swimmer!" From the first we were horrified of the water, and sank like a stone whenever placed in it. Later it was suggested that we were built like a tennis player. The result of this build was one love set after another, with us representing the love interest.

In our teens, we went briefly to sea, in a sailboat. Sailboats are prettier from the seashore than they are in the sea. We found that in sailing, you must "come about" constantly, and this involves strenuous ducking to avoid the boom, which inevitably butts you in the head. There was real hope of horsemanship, and we did well at this until we got a job teaching riding at summer camp. Then we showed the white feather, when it was pointed out to us that the small paying guests must ride the safe horses. The instructors, who contributed nothing to camp support, were logical sacrifices to the dangerous horses who bucked, reared or ran away.

All in all, it looked like croquet might be our cup of tea, until we heard about golf. We took up golf, we had a few lessons and started out happily with a group of beginners.

That was ten years ago, and we have about run out of beginners. Ladies who learned with us are now champions. Beginners of today were toddlers when we first addressed the ball. We have made a record of sorts, but it is not the sort we had in mind. Many a golfer has swung at the ball and missed, but few have shot the ball over his shoulder and to the rear. We once even hit the club champion, in the longest and most unexpected shot of our life. But we never could break 100, on nine, that is.

This became a terrific psychological handicap, and

threatened our inner poise. We must break 100, we told ourself. If we don't break 100, we continued, we may never succeed at anything.

We have at last broken 100 and we will tell you how we did it. If you can't break 100 on nine, girls, try three. We have finally struck our stride. Three holes on a hot afternoon is enough, and our score has considerably improved. So any day now, we may trot out to a nearby course, and swing merrily down the rough, knowing that the fight will not be long, the score will not be large, and the suntan will be just as authentic as if we were Patty Berg.

Planning to Build?

AS THE RING of the carpenter's hammer makes mighty music in the morning air, our heart goes out to builders of homes. This spring, more than ever before, houses will rise in our town, on hill and dale, by spring and lake, near bus-stop and super-market. They will be long and low and short and fat; they will be contemporary and they will be traditional, they will be conditioned against heat and cold and termites and small children, and a good many of them will be mortgaged to the hilt.

But this is not why our heart goes out to builders of homes. Our heart goes out because of the stresses they will undergo before they stumble across the threshold, home-owners at last.

If they think, poor innocents, that they can build a home just like they want it, with no cheering from the sidelines, they are mistaken. They are about to undergo the most intensive barrage of advice from close friends and total strangers that it is possible to imagine. Most of them cannot imagine it. Therefore, we feel that we should prepare them for the inevitable advance of the experts.

Unsolicited volunteers will testify that it is best to build with an architect, without an architect, with a contractor, without a contractor, on a cost plus basis, with a lock and key contract, and without any help at all, except from close personal friends who also happen to be carpenters.

They will learn that a wood kitchen is better than a metal kitchen, and that a metal kitchen is better than a wood kitchen, and that some people in Florida cook outdoors all year, equipped with only a few tin cans and a cigarette lighter. They will be told that in Jackson it is best to float a foundation on a concrete slab and to go down to China on wood piling.

They will find, after they have signed a contract, that they have signed the wrong kind of contract. They will learn, after they have hired a builder, that they hired the wrong builder. They will listen, with quivering chins, to harrowing personal experiences, told by friends whose roofs fell suddenly down about their ears, or whose plumbing erupted during a dinner party for ten.

They will go through all this, and more besides, before that happy day when they can call their home their own. Then, shattered by suggestion and harassed by doubts, they can collapse in their own living room, and plan a few well-chosen remarks with which to regale unsuspecting friends who are planning to build.

There Go the Joneses

THE JONESES ARE hard people to keep up with. Time was when they entertained their friends in the family dining room, with fried chicken, rice and gravy, peas and mushrooms, hot biscuits, and ice cream with chocolate sauce, for company dinner. This pattern persisted until someone noticed the beauties of nature, and almost simultaneously scientists dealt death to night-flying insects, with the discovery of DDT. Forthwith the Joneses, long an indoor group, moved outdoors.

The move involved outdoor furniture, which in the beginning of the patio phase was rustic, and a great deal of marching back and forth bearing potato salad. To eliminate the marching, barbecue pits sprung up like mushrooms, and a great deal of marching back and forth bearing beeves or burgers took place.

About now the Boston Cookbook went out the window, and the garden vegetables stayed underground. Casseroles bloomed into prominence, and new sets of bright-colored crockery sounded the knell for Mother's Haviland. The old boiled dinner became a memory, and if the entree wasn't roped on the last roundup, skewered and thrown bodily into a blazing fire, the party was dull. Holes were dug in which to cook corn in its shuck, clams in their shells, and Father on his fingers, and the whole affair began to look like Home on the Range.

At this approximate point, someone went to California, and brought back the word that patios had there attained a suave peak of perfection. Outdoor furniture became smarter, more functional, more expensive. African camp chairs appeared to supplant the old Morris, and wrought iron began its insidious grip on the furniture industry.

Now a whole new wardrobe was involved in the patio party, and Mother laid aside her good crepe dress and stumbled into loafers. Father, normally in Oxford grey, got into the spirit of things in a brilliant sports shirt. In some extreme instances, he wore a chef's cap and an apron emblazoned with tired wit.

In an effort to keep up with the Joneses, miles of brick were laid, and patios blossomed like the rose. Plants, said to be especially congenial with borders and brick, were set out in profusion, and all kinds of cooking equipment went into the new establishment. Villainous knives and long-handled forks joined the vast list of outdoor cooking equipment, and old lanterns were hauled out, refurbished, and filled with kerosene, as time turned back for the Joneses and their guests.

About the time some of us laboriously laid the last brick, and stood back panting to survey the scene of our future social triumphs, the malevolent whirring of an air-conditioning motor broke the summer spell.

"Ho, hum," said the Joneses, brought up in the family dining room, nurtured on many a moonlit potato salad, "We can't ask anyone to sit outside in this heat. After all, they're used to air-conditioning." So saying, they put back on their coats and marched indoors, leaving us confounded, defeated, and at long last ready to dine on the patio.

Apartment for Rent

Apartment for Rent

HOME IS WHERE the heart is. In my case, it is where the tenants are also. This union of heart and tenants results in both joys and sorrows. Let me tell you about some of the sorrows.

On a winter's day I had a telephone call from my upstairs tenant. This is a bad sign. "The refrigerator is off," he announced, "and everything in it is spoiling." I rejected an unworthy mental picture of everything in it, which I happened to know was a TV dinner, and assumed my responsibility. I suggested that he call an electrician.

Some time and a good many conversations later I went home, shifted the TV dinner to my own refrigerator, and hoped that the electrician would come in his own good time, fix the refrigerator, and leave us in peace. Not at all.

The next chilly day I was in my office where I belong, and again the voice of the tenant was heard on the line. There was a new note of urgency in his voice. "The refrigerator is fixed," he said, "but the electrician fell through the ceiling."

Years of landladyship having made me pessimistic, I asked, "Is he dead?"

"No, he isn't hurt," the tenant said, "but there is a big hole in the ceiling and I may freeze."

All of this is very shattering to the working person, but I knew where my duty lay. I came home and got on the line to the contractor. Days later, after enforced association with sheetrock people, tapers, sanders and painters, the tenant had a working refrigerator, a neat ceiling, and his TV dinner back where it belonged. All seemed well on Hackberry Hill, which is a euphemism for where we live.

"Somewhere," I thought foolishly, "the sun is shining."

On a Saturday night I came in late, and heard sounds of revelry emanating from the apartment of my upstairs tenant. "Come back here," he called as I made a beeline for my boudoir. Taking this for a social invitation, I declined graciously. "Thanks so much," I said, "but I'm sleepy and I'm going to bed."

"You'd better come back here," he said, again that note of urgency I had begun to fear. "Water is dripping through my floor into Martha's apartment."

This is just the kind of news a landlady needs most at eleven o'clock on a Saturday night. Martha is one half of the downstairs tenants, the other half at that time being in Vietnam. Again there was no escape from responsibility. I went back to the upstairs tenant's apartment, where I found a jolly group, some in morning coats, still celebrating what must have been a noon wedding. I made the trip downstairs with my upstairs tenant, and sure enough, water was dripping right through the ceiling into Martha's apartment.

The problem seemed insoluble, at that time and place, but John, the upstairs tenant, and I stumbled into the dark recesses of the basement looking for a water cutoff. Finding none, we formed a bucket brigade. Once John and I had buckets under the most effusive leaks he returned to his guests, who were delighted with the mysterious flood. I gave thanks that Martha was out of town, and withdrew to tackle the Yellow Pages in search of a plumber.

I soon found out that "24-hour plumbers" do not consider eleven-thirty on Saturday night one of the hours. Between eleven-thirty and midnight I talked to a number of interesting telephone personalities, but made no useful contacts. One plumber said in a husky voice, "Well, hon, it just isn't convenient for anyone to come on Saturday night." Another took his phone off the hook after suggesting that I call back in a few minutes. The company which advertised itself as the "big, nationwide company, no job too big, no job too small," apparently did not think of us as part of the nation. A plumber's wife said her husband was at the Golden Gloves and should have been home thirty minutes ago. So it went, midnight struck, John's guests left, we had been up and down the steps a dozen times, and the drip-drip-drip of the unidentified leak was getting more like splash-splash-splash. At 12:35 a.m., I located a real 24-hour plumber, who came grudgingly, but who came.

He tore up the floors in both the upstairs and downstairs apartments, located a broken pipe, checked the hot-water heater and said with his first indication of enthusiasm, "This here's just about corroded, ma'am, and when it goes, it really goes!" and refused to leave without collecting on the spot. "I been told not to leave until you pay cash," he said firmly and insultingly.

It took me a few weeks to get over the shock of buying a new hot-water heater and having the broken pipe replaced, but I was doing very well when the downstairs tenant knocked a hole in the kitchen wall.

I should explain at this point that my tenants are very gentlemanly and ladylike personalities, harmless and helpful in ordinary circumstances. But there is something about my rental property that invites disaster. The downstairs tenants, reunited upon Bowden's return from Vietnam, decided to purchase a new refrigerator. I threw in the old refrigerator as a gesture of good will to the United States Marines, and all went well until the new refrigerator was delivered. The moving man who delivered the refrigerator kept on moving after he got into the tiny kitchen, and pushed the new refrigerator right through the kitchen wall. A gaping hole downstairs took the place of the gaping hole upstairs, and once more my rendezvous with the world of construction became inevitable. After a couple of conferences with sheetrock people, tapers, sanders and painters, I realized that my health would not survive another building project. I gave the downstairs tenants an ultimatum which could be roughly translated as, "It's all yours, baby," and it still is. In the summertime I hope the hole in the kitchen wall provides nice additional ventilation.

We have gotten along extremely well since these crises. The only ripple on the calm surface of our relationship came the other day when Martha asked me to let her in her apartment, as she had misplaced her key. We all misplace our keys from time to time, so this was no cause for alarm. However, I had just gotten home from a hard day, had taken off my shoes and my dress, and had collapsed on the sofa. I dragged myself up in this state of undress, went through the upstairs apartment to the downstairs door, let Martha in, came back upstairs, and found the door from my house into John's apartment had slammed shut and locked behind me. I was locked in my male tenant's apartment, barefoot and clad only in my slip. I made a rough calculation as to how I could get along without the rent, found I couldn't make it, and went back downstairs for help. Martha was cooperative, together we tried to break into the house, and finally succeeded in knocking an air conditioner askew and crawling in a window.

These, as I have said, are some of the sorrows of home. Some of the joys are when the tenants do not break anything, but instead bring bream and white perch from a fishing trip, or fresh vegetables from a visit home, or potables from the potable store, and visit in the twilight, exchanging horror stories about the hazards of living with me. I always point out that I do not charge anything extra for the wild life, and the swallow that cheeps in their chimney is free.

The Tiny Tenant

YOU'RE NEVER TOO OLD to learn. For example, we have learned a lesson from a baby. The lesson is that in dealing with a baby, the baby makes the rules. For years we have felt that a conversation carried on in baby talk is unnecessary, even degrading. Why, we reasoned, isn't it possible for grown people to speak pleasantly, even affectionately, to a baby in English? Why wouldn't a baby be just as glad to hear, "Good morning baby, I love you, you are so sweet," as "Dood mownin' babee, I oove oo, oo toe tweet."

The fact is, he isn't, and we don't know why. Possibly in the Everywhere out of which babies come, the conversation is carried on in some strange patois that is most closely approximated on earth by baby talk.

The reason we know this is that a six weeks old baby rents from us. We are fond of the little fellow, and we have tried to be friendly with him. "Hi, baby," we have said, cheerily. "You're a nice baby, you're a good boy." With this he tucks his mouth down at the corners, pokes out his lower lip, and stares reproachfully at us. His eyes grow big and his tiny brow knits in a frown.

This frightens us, and we retreat hastily into the time-honored device.

"Dood mowning' oo feet fing," we amend our statement. "Hey-o, hey-o!" Now this is what he had in mind all along. This he understands. His mouth spreads in a broad grin, he drools appreciatively, waves his hands, and kicks one foot. "Hey-o," he says back, and do you know, we really think he does.

Of course anybody knows that a six weeks old baby can't even focus, much less talk. But he can certainly lay down the law, and he knows what he will tolerate in the way of conversation. Anything less than adoration, and that high-pitched, bores him. So we have been forced to give up our well laid plans to speak English to our tiny tenant. We'll even do business with him on his own terms, if he insists, and tell him if he isn't a dood boy the went may doe way up.

By the Dawn's Early Light

A GOOD MANY PEOPLE have asked us what happened to the baby. That is, our tiny tenant who inspired us to a couple of dewy-eyed columns filled with vivid descriptions of two-month-old precocity. We haven't written anything about him now for some months, and it seems that he has a public avid to hear about him.

Frankly, the first rift has come between us. Without saying a word to anybody, he put himself on daylight saving time. Now at five in the morning, with the first straggling gray of day in the sky, the tiny tenant lifts his pretty head and makes a statement. The statement is monotonous in the extreme, plaintive, insistent, and comes mighty early in the morning. His room is just under our own boudoir, and without any effort at all he breaks the sound barrier.

The baby doesn't exactly cry. It's more like a bark. He says the same thing over and over, from around five to about eight-thirty, and it goes something like this: "uh-wuh, uh-wuh, uh-wuh, uh-wuh." Somehow we don't think this is as smart as some other statements he may make at a brighter time of the day.

Some mornings, worn and torn with the vicissitudes of the lady wage earner who also goes forth into some fairly late nights, we could pinch the little fellow's head off. Instead, we lie rigid in our bed, grip the sheets, and wait for one or both of his parents to do something. The parents, young, strong, and apparently deaf, often sleep right through it. When we can stand it no longer, we hurl back the covers, stumble out of bed, and in the cold gray dawn tiptoe downstairs, prepared to do murder.

Instead, in a few minutes we are back in bed, and with a friend. The baby has won again. Our arrival was just what he had in mind, and he greets us with a cheer.

He smiles, drools, kicks with enthusiasm, and beats his bed with his fists. Nobody else is that carried away with us. Of course he is just that carried away with anyone he sees at five a.m., but his chances seem best to see us. So he joins us in bed, every now and then chuckling triumphantly, and patting us at random with a very wet fist which he keeps in his mouth for just such occasions.

How to Get a Baby

"YOU DON'T STILL write Miss Quote, do you?" we were asked by a nice red-headed young man who purports to read us. "Why?" we countered. "It just doesn't sound like you," he said. "Better or worse?" we asked. "It's not that," he answered, "It's just that the person who writes it now has a baby."

Well, it looks as if we'd better clear this up. There are all kinds of ways to have a baby. You can have one, in the old-fashioned biological sense of the word, one can be given you, you can get one. We've got one. We did not have it, it was not given us, we certainly didn't ask for it, but we've got it. It's a boy, two months old, and he rents from us.

This is how you can tell when you've got a baby.

When you are proud that his head wobbles without falling off, you've got one. When you tell guests to drop by at the midnight feeding, because that is when he laughs out loud, you've got one. When you think it is brilliant that he admires his hands all day, you've got one. When you report seriously that at two months he is saying a few words, you've got one. When you compare progress notes with his contemporaries, and note how advanced he is, you've got one. When you carefully brush his perfectly bald head so he will look his best, you've got one.

So, nice red-headed young man, here's your answer. We do write Miss Quote, and we've got a baby. On second thought, maybe the baby's got us.

The Little Wrecker

THERE IS A BABY bulldozer in our home. It occurs to us, that with his superior talents for demolition, we might make a deal with his parents to rent him out on a commission basis. We note that where there is a lot of building, there is also a lot of tearing down. This is especially so in commercial districts, where old buildings are wrecked to make way for new ones. After watching the little wrecker in our home, we are convinced that he has a great future, if we can get by the child labor law.

Our idea is that this small, light and extremely maneuverable wrecker could save untold time and money in demolishing unwanted or obsolete property. This would be a move in the right direction, for he is currently engaged in demolishing property that is neither unwanted nor obsolete. Take a look at this tiny terror, as he goes about his business with utter absorption. At nine months, he weighs twenty pounds, and is equipped with four teeth which act as scoops in his work. He is economical to operate, as he subsists in part on the material he wrecks. Old newspapers, bits of carpet, drapery material, bones and bottles delight his soul and thrill his palate, and are second only to electric light wires and telephone cords in his esteem.

As for performance, if you will set him down and give him his head in a fully equipped living room, we guarantee he will have it clean as a whistle in five minutes flat. He is an efficient little thing, and works with a master plan or schedule. He destroys fragile objects first, making a beeline for china, ceramics and crystal. These he fondles, chews and then dashes to the floor, making a whale of a mess. It is best to dissuade him from eating the remnants there, as we have found that paper material is better on his digestion.

After the breakables which he breaks, he attacks the unbreakables, which he also breaks. High on his list of favorites are potted plants. Leaves he loves to chew and pluck, or vice versa. After the leaves are thoroughly chewed, the plant is bent until it gives up the ghost, if its stem is not a crisp type. To finish the job, pot and wounded plant are hurled to the floor, and the baby bulldozer moves systematically on to his next task.

If you have a coffee table, with the conventional collection of ash trays, magazines, books, fruit or flowers, as we do, the tiny terror begins carefully at one corner, and in a trice the table is bare. The ash trays are easily disposed of, the magazines and books are chewed or rent asunder, and we don't know exactly what he does with the fruit, as we are still looking for an artificial lemon.

So if you need some wrecking done, we have a candidate. If not, don't invite the baby bulldozer to call, unless you specify that his mother hold him firmly on her lap, while his glittering eye takes in the joyful possibilities of new worlds to conquer and new decor to destroy.

La Mere Goose

TODAY WE ARE SPEECHLESS. We make a statement, and no sound comes. For once the virus is not the villain. Back of this depressing state of affairs is Little Tommy Tucker. Back of Little Tommy Tucker are Bo Peep, Little Boy Blue, Old King Cole, and a host of fabled characters who follow in the train of La Mere Goose.

And back of them all is the Tiny Tenant, man of the year in this department. As the Tiny Tenant has built up a following, and as his fans are constantly clamoring for word of him, we feel justified in making this report. For those who came in late, the Tiny Tenant is thirteen months old and rents from us. Our association is very close, in spite of all we can do, and he has proved useful to us as material for our career.

Back to La Mere Goose. Seeing the Tiny Tenant stand bemused in front of the television set, we once said firmly and thoughtlessly to his mother: "I hope the child will like books. I hope he will like to read."

Because someone gave the Tiny Tenant a linen bound copy of Mother Goose. Turns out he is mad for books, and wild about reading. The only thing is, he can't read. So naturally he turns to someone who can. When he presses Mother Goose, bound in linen, upon his mother, with an urgent statement in Russian which translated means "Read to me," his mother, remembering like a crafty elephant, says to him: "Take the book to Aunt Quote. Aunt Quote loves to read. Aunt Quote wants you to love to read. Take the book to Aunt Quote."

The upshot of all this is that far into the gloaming, we are all tied up with Tommy Tucker and his supper song,

Bo Peep and her wandering sheep, Old King Cole and his fiddlers three, and the Old Goose herself, who is behind this overtime work without pay.

For years proud mothers have told us in wondering tones that their little people are able to recite Mother Goose rhymes without prompting. For years we thought that was pretty smart. But now we know that any child who "loves books, loves to read," and who can't recite Mother Goose rhymes without prompting should have his little head examined.

After all, Tiny Tenant hears Tommy Tucker about one hundred times every day. Soon, we trust, he can tell the Tucker story himself, without prompting. And soon, we trust, our ragged vocal chords worn with constant repetition of the immortal jingles of childhood, can rest, and we can watch television.

Out of the Nowhere

YOU HEAR A LOT about cruel landlords. There are, of course, two sides to this story. We cannot speak for landlords, but we know a great deal about landladies. We are one, as a matter of fact, in a small way. And to a landlady in a small way, anything can happen.

For example, you can rent to two people, and then suddenly without a word of warning, there are three. This is exactly what happened to us. The third renter came to us from out of the nowhere, but he is certainly into the here in a big way, eighteen months later.

To landladies who are expecting, through no fault of their own, we have a word of warning. Build and decorate with natural materials. Like wood, stone, brick or concrete. A baby, being the most natural material, is very hard on any material which is not natural.

Take wallpaper. If you don't, the baby will. The tenant in our apartment, now eighteen months old and mighty busy, has stripped the entrance hall of wallpaper, slowly, methodically, and with total success. When apprehended in this act of violence, he shakes his head and murmurs reproachfully, "Oh, Dan. Mess." As if he were neither Dan nor a party to the mess.

Take plumbing. We understand that plumbing is a baby's chief delight in all homes. Certainly in our apartment, the baby's favorite plaything is the plumbing. He puts into it all manner of valuables, including himself.

Whenever there is a moment of silence, we dash for the plumbing. There we find an odd flotilla, in imminent danger of being swept into the sewer. Pacifiers, car keys, cigarette lighters, pictures, combs, toothbrushes and kitchen utensils are our tenant's favorite water toys. He especially likes to get in with them, and at times adds toast to the mixture, to be retrieved when properly damp.

We finally persuaded the baby's mother that at eighteen months, he is entitled to some plumbing of his own, Dr. Spock to the contrary notwithstanding. Accordingly, she purchased some equipment recommended for the growing youth, but this purchase has been a total failure. The baby thinks it is a hat, and wears it on his head all day. This confusion could lead to all sorts of disasters, and as we say, the landlady's lot is fraught with peril.

Landladies, worn and torn from the stresses of making property pay, are surely entitled to a quiet cup of coffee in the evening. The baby in our property is against drinking—anything. We know this because in a macabre moment he broke us of the coffee habit.

We boiled some water, got out the drip coffee pot, put the required amount of coffee in it, poured the boiling water in, and in due time got a cup of coffee. After the first sip, with tiny pursed lips we called for help.

An investigation revealed that the baby, on his daily rounds of our own apartment, had filled the bottom of the coffee pot with Dutch Cleanser. The combination is guaranteed to put you on Pearl River water for life.

As we say, it's a hard life, being a landlady to a baby. The only thing that makes it pay is that an eighteen-month-old baby can smile sweeter, and laugh happier, and hug you tighter, than anything else you could possibly get to tear down your apartment.

Summer is for Children

SUMMER IS FOR CHILDREN. I know because I have a friend who is five years old. She has lost two teeth, another is loose, and she can dial her telephone number. By these signs she knows that she is getting big.

Another sign is that in the fall she will be scrubbed clean, her hair will be brushed until it shines, she will put on a dark cotton dress, black patent shoes and white socks, and she will present herself to Elementary Education.

Meanwhile, she has Summer. This is a time of playing out, begging to go swimming, going swimming, begging to play in the hose, playing in the hose, and dispensing hospitality to her friends, who tramp through the house all day long bringing souvenirs of summer rains, and whose trips to the refrigerator cannot be numbered.

Her friends range in age from four to six, and the youngest boy, a handsome devil, bites. In the sub-school set this is frowned upon, but quickly forgiven.

Hospitality consists of cookies galore, sweet soft drinks in poisonous colors, and sugary confections in the shape of trolls and bats. Outside, the play continues: freeze tag, chase, and hide-and-go-seek in the long summer afternoons.

My friend loves her father most, needs her mother most, and worries her brothers most. Her father calls her sweetheart, her brothers call her Stupid, and her mother calls her and calls her.

Right now she wishes she was a boy. A couple of weeks ago she loved being a girl. She may present herself *au naturel* in the living room when company is present, or she may have a fit of modesty if you chance upon her in the tub. She would rather wear her Batman shirt than any party dress in her closet.

She doesn't care too much for dolls and tea sets since her brothers introduced her to a gamier world of squirt guns and space shots. She represents a vast consumer market for television inspired junk, and the nicest thing she can give you is a set of ugly stickers.

This child believes in Santa Claus because she has heard his reindeer on her roof, and she believes in the Easter bunny because she heard him, too, in the bushes outside her window.

She believes in the fairy who left her a quarter for her first tooth, and she knows that this fairy can read because she lost the next tooth and still collected when her father left a note of explanation.

When she goes swimming with the family, she spends most of her time on the bottom of the pool. Therefore she smells of chlorine, as well as grass and cookies, and on occasion, worse. At night she is clean, and the sweet smell of Soaky hovers over her bed.

She can't wait. Not for anything. "Come out and

play!" or "Come and watch television!" call for immediate action. "Just a minute!" won't do the job. For she says, "Oh, a minute's *long!*"

And you, who know that a year is short, hurry because she says "Come *on!*"

She still has the tag end of summer ahead of her, and she'll make the most of it. Her parents will wonder if she'll ever stop talking or if she'll ever stop slamming the refrigerator door, but they'll make the most of it too. For they know that this special time is short, in a twinkling summer will be over, a school door will open, and a little girl will walk away.

The silence will be deafening.

Fasten Your Seat Belts

What, la Peste?

WE ARE STANDING with reluctant feet where the brook
and the Atlantic Ocean meet, for having read with
mounting excitement that this is the first summer we
can fly to Europe on the installment plan, we are on our
way.

We make this announcement in the public press not
because it is in any way newsworthy, but because we
are going to take off for a week or so, and we want our
readers to remain true blue during our holiday.

The reason that our feet are reluctant is that some
necessary preparations for overseas flight have de-
pressed us. There is our International Health
Certificate, for example, which speaks of la variole,
(smallpox to you), la fievre jaune, le cholera, et of all
things, le peste, in four languages. As if this weren't
discouraging enough, the U. S. State Department has
sent us a helpful booklet on how to get home if dead.
While we are sure this is a project we will never have to
engineer personally, it is a sobering thought.

We have also received alluring advertisements from
friends in the insurance business, which point out
splendid benefits for loss of head, and all other mem-

bers, and a good many non-members, excepting dental plates and pet animals, while travelling abroad. This has made no change in our plans for carrying an animal abroad, but we will surely double-check our dental plate.

Last blow at this writing is an excellent book on travel in Europe, which cheerily advises, "Don't forget your airplane insurance at takeoff time! It may be the best investment you ever made!"

To counteract the pall that has been cast about our great skyfaring adventure, we murmur manfully over and over enchanting names like the River Arno and the Tuscan Hills, the Champs Elysees and the Ponte Veccio, the Jungfrau and the Matterhorn, the Campagna Romano and the Spanish Steps. If it all turns out for the best, we may toss a coin in that Roman fountain. But at the moment, we are making the most of the glorious fourth, an old American holiday we appreciate more and more as time goes by.

Fasten Your Seat Belts

Paris, July 14, 1954
FIRST, A WORD on the age of flight. Charles Lindbergh

in the *Spirit of St. Louis,* some years back, was probably not nearly so nervous as I, settling into the TWA Constellation called *Star of Nebraska,* that was to whisk us through time and space and deposit us at Orly Field in little more time than it takes to say Jacques Robinson. However, for tourists contemplating such a flight, I testify that it ain't bad at all. Having a sack full of sleeping pills helped, for Ruth Forbes, my companion of the voyage, and I applied the barbiturates at Gander, Newfoundland, and came to in Paris. Before the Federal narcotics agents close in on me, let me add that I recommend such measures only for transatlantic flight.

We checked into the Continental, a lovely hotel located just across the Garden of the Tuileries from the Seine, around the corner from the Place Vendome, and a hop, skip and jump from the Place de la Concorde, where Marie Antoinette lost her pretty head. Here we wallowed in the unaccustomed splendor of our hotel room, which had crystal chandeliers, a giant bathroom, wonderful toweling bathrobes, and a view of the incinerator. It has been my experience that hotel room clerks inevitably assign single lady travelers to this view, which is available everywhere.

Having studied several travel guides, including Art Buchwald's *Paris After Dark,* we rose above guided tours, and set forth on foot to investigate Paris. The results were fairly rewarding, except to the feet. The limits of space and the patience of our readers confine me to report without detail that we did just about everything that all tourists do, including dining in splendor at Maxim's and Tour d'Argent, where we were seated behind a post and managed to get a snack for eleven dollars. We had tea at the Continental, cinzano and soda at the Café de la Paix, patisseries at Fouquet's on the Champs Elysées, and best of all, beer and peanuts by the lake in the Bois de Boulogne. In spite of our reading material Paris after dark seemed to be too much for us, so we joined the night club tour and saw the semi-stripped ladies of Paris, who are fairly conservative nowadays and wear everything but tops.

Our favorite thing was a boat ride on the Seine in a bateau mouche. This is not a tour, no guide pontificates, the riders are mostly French, and the cheap voyage glides by Notre Dame and the Ile de St. Louis, under the gorgeous bridges of the Seine, and past the landmarks of Paris to the village of St. Cloud. After two hours on the river we had a good idea of the plan of the city, and we even made friends with a French couple. At least, we thought we did, but we were never sure, as we made halting conversation based on our French phrase book. This book must have been written by an irritable tourist, as it includes only phrases of complaint, like "the dishes are dirty," and "how can you prove to me that you are reliable?" The French couple smiled happily and occasionally laughed wildly, so we felt that our phrases were not as bad as they might have been.

Now for my confession. I suppose that I am the only American who ever went to Paris and did not visit the Louvre. This unforgivable omission was quite unavoidable, for I neglected to check a calendar of French holidays, and somehow failed to realize that July 14 is

Bastille Day, the great French national holiday, and the Louvre is *très fermé.* In our careful planning we had saved the best for last, which is today. Tonight we take the Orient Express for Lucerne, after which all roads lead to Rome.

Failing in our cultural mission to admire the *Mona Lisa* and her companion masterworks, we decided to take in the Bastille Day parade. This was my second Parisian mistake. I took up a position in the Louvre gardens, before the Arc de Triomphe du Carrousel. The parade was magnificent, seemed to go on for hours, and included French Foreign Legionnaires, mounted troops, cadets from military schools, the Army, the Air Force, and the Navy, all in dress uniform including plumes and swords. Horses pranced, bands played, drums beat, flags waved, and then the parade broke up, right at the Arc. The result was that I was trapped in a swirling mass of French military might, all apparently determined that I should not pass. This made it impossible for me to rejoin Miss Forbes, and set off a panic within me for fear that I could not get out of the armed forces in time to catch the Orient Express. As you can tell, I did get out, and I shall always remember Bastille Day, right along with the Fourth of July.

Florence, July 24, 1954
We have been asked why, on our brief introductory tour of Europe, we chose Florence as one of our three stops. We reasoned that if Florence was good enough for Michelangelo, Galileo, da Vinci and Botticelli, to say nothing of the Medici popes and princes, it was good

enough for us. Actually, we hoped to derive some artistic inspiration from the City of the Lily, but here we are, still writing "Miss Quote."

A note on European trains may be in order. When it is announced that a European, or specifically an Italian, train will leave the station at so many seconds past so many minutes past such and such an hour, it means it; Italian trains also arrive on schedule. Therefore, it is well for a tourist in Italy to be alert, sound of wind and limb, and ready to leap either on or off. I would put our Italian electric train in the class with TWA's *Star of Nebraska* for excitement. It may go faster. We had a mad ride down the Alps to Italy, over the Gotthard Pass, by Lake Como and Milano, past the turrets of walled villages, and through olive groves on softly green hills. The train paused in Florence only long enough to deposit us in the cradle of the arts, and then rushed on toward Rome.

We were well located in the Savoy Hotel on the busy Piazza della Repubblica, with a view of the hotel incinerator. This was to be expected, but we also had access to a balcony which overlooked the Piazza. Here the Italians and the tourists gather, music is played and sung far into the night, and snatches of grand opera issue surprisingly from the throats of happy diners and drinkers. And here we made our most serious European mistake.

Charmed by our overview of the magnificent square, which was dominated by a Romanesque arch and animated by Gilli's sidewalk cafe, we rushed right down to Gilli's, and decided to start off our look at Florence with a Florentine libation. A smiling waiter appeared, and asked, "Would madame care for an aperitif?" Overcome by local color I said, "Yes, your specialty, please." Miss Forbes, wiser and a second-time tourist, stuck to Scotch. The waiter was especially pleased with me, however, and returned to our table promptly, bearing the pale and innocent-looking whisky with a sinister beverage of darker hue. "What's that?" I asked. "A negroni!" he proclaimed proudly. "Our specialty!" With some apprehension we downed the negroni, and only when we took sodium pentothal for our one and only operation have we been similarly affected. Circulation seemed to stop from our wrists up, and if we had been offered ten thousand lire (not much, really) to move, we couldn't have done it. Bravely continental to the end, we worked our way through the negroni, and the next day we seriously considered joining Elizabeth Barrett Browning in the Protestant Cemetery in Florence.

From that day forward our banners were blazoned with beef, bourbon, and bicarbonate, and try to get any of them in Italy. In spite of this temporary setback, we pressed forward, and after a day of rest and recuperation in the Savoy we were able to totter through the Uffizi Palace, where many of the world's great masterpieces are hung, and the Bargello Palace, notable for its sculptures which include the *Flying Mercury* and Donatello's *St. George*.

After this exposure to art we took a late afternoon carriage ride across the Arno and into the Tuscan hills to the Piazza Michelangelo, a beautiful square honoring the great Florentine, where a reproduction of his mighty

David surveys the valley below. Still higher in the hills is the ancient church of San Miniato, and from this lofty eminence we saw a sunset that turned the Arno to gold, cast purple shadows on the Duomo and the Campanile, and put the masterpieces of the Uffizi far in the shade.

Shopping in Florence is fine but not cheap, and with the dollar worth about 650 lire, you need a sack for your change. Dining is fine too, and we liked best ravioli at Alfredo's sidewalk cafe and minestrone and chicken cacciatore at Doney's restaurant. Pleasant surprise was the Italian enthusiasm for iced tea, with the world's largest slice of lemon. I found this very beneficial after the negroni.

For our friends who might like to call on us when we get home, but are afraid we will show them our slides, we have encouraging news. We haven't any slides. As we leave Florence we have only three pictures, all taken by itinerant photographers who batten on tourists, and they may be seen in a trice.

Rome, July 28, 1954

With the full realization that we really don't know much about Europe after two weeks abroad, but happy to have something different to say, we now make our final foreign report. Last stages of our itinerary went something like Rome and then Home, and as we left Florence we were ready for both. In Rome we checked into the Grand Hotel, which is most grand and mighty old, though by Roman standards, it is still a pup. Had we dreamt that we dwelt in marble halls, we never could have dreamt up so much marble. Of all the splendid bathrooms we found in Europe, the Grand has the most splendid of all, with marble simply everywhere and room for a small tea dance. The Grand was reserved for diplomats during World War II, so we felt that we had a good address, if only we could find someone to give it to.

This is where the *Rome Daily American* came to our rescue, with its daily listing of new hotel arrivals in Rome. Happily for us, young Tom Crockett, a home town boy abroad, read the listing which noted our arrival, and called us at once. Tom and his Harvard roommate put in a full day with us and at day's end had dropped their polite "yes ma'ams" and were jammed into a carriage with us going at a great gallop up the Via Vittorio Veneto headed for supper at the Hotel Flora.

Earlier in the day we had lunch at Tre Scalini, visited the Pantheon, the Roman Forum and the Forum of Julius Caesar, took two pictures at the Colosseum, and saw the column of Trajan and the Piazza Venezia where Mussolini shouted his way to fame and death. On the Appian Way, I half expected Ben Hur to burst forth and join us at full gallop, one foot on each chariot. Later, at the Flora, popular rendezvous for Americans in Rome, we had antipasto in its finest form, and lamb chops, not too characteristic but mighty delicious.

The Vatican needs no amplification from us. We did struggle around to buy the scarves required to cover our bare heads and hot bare arms before entering St. Peter's. The *Pieta* remains with me as the most moving sculpture I have ever seen; another tremendous experience was Michelangelo's ceiling in the Sistine Chapel, where white smoke rises through a slender flue to announce the election of popes. I like the story about Michelangelo's splendid revenge on a Master of Ceremonies to Pope Paul II, who protested against the nudity of some of his figures in the Sistine Chapel. Michelangelo simply included the Master's face in Hell, graced with ass's ears.

Our best evening was spent at the Baths of Caracalla, where among the ancient ruins of the emperor's public baths an open-air theater has been built, and summer opera continues through August. We heard *Carmen* there, and the combination of the ruins, the music, and overhead the stars of heaven and the twinkle of the lights on an occasional airplane gave us plenty to think about.

En route home our plane was in a queue circling over New York for so long we were almost out of gas, and the captain gave us the choice of landing in Boston or Montreal. We took Boston, and spent a night at the Parker House in our petticoats. Now home again, we have been asked for advice on foreign travel, which is undeserved flattery. "What did you take for two weeks?" we are asked. "What did you need most over there?" What we took and what we needed were two different things. We took a wool suit, two cotton suits and a black dress, and what we needed most was a man. If you can arrange the combination, you will be better off.

Westward the Women

THIS IS A STORY with a moral, and the moral has to do with grass being greener on the other side of the fence, and a black hard-top Cadillac convertible being more desirable if you're not driving it 1,500 miles due west. To begin at the beginning, which is the best possible place, let us say that we still would like to have a black hard-top Cadillac convertible of our very own, one we had nurtured from its childhood and one whose habits we understood. But to be transferred suddenly from the quiet comfort of a Plymouth whose habits we do understand to the powerpacked mysteries of a used Cadillac, which makes it more mysterious, was almost too much for our economically deprived system.

The story is that our venturesome cousins, Susan and Vicki, told us they had a deal to drive a Cadillac to the West Coast, all expenses paid, and they asked us to come along. What they didn't tell us was that the Cadillac had lived long and hard before it met us, and that the expenses were to be borne by us, after all, including the purchase of a lady truck driver's license in New Mexico.

To get on with the story, which is almost as long as

the trip, we three ladies flew low out of Memphis on a fine April morning, living a lie. People whistled at us who wouldn't have tipped their hat to us in our Plymouth. We whirred and purred into Arkansas, and in Palestine, Arkansas, still on a fine April morning, and about an hour out of Memphis, we clanged to a stop. This was the first of many forced landings, during which we learned to know and love the countryside and to hate the Cadillac.

Had it not been for a knight of the road, driving an oil-burning truck, we might be writing this from Palestine, Arkansas, on a fine May morning. But our hero roared by in a cloud of smoke, took in the situation, and paused to assist us. This he did, diagnosing our difficulty as motor muck. During the diagnosis we became so close he almost joined our party, but when we three maiden ladies told him our husbands were waiting for us in California he went on with his load of rice.

Things became tenser as we skimmed into Texas, for the spectre of motor muck hovered over the speedometer. A night's lodging in Dallas brightened us up, as any Texan will understand, and refreshed in mind and body, with a false sense of security, we hummed toward Fort Worth, where we were arrested for humming more than forty miles an hour.

It was in Texas that the rock hit the windshield, shattering it. This was no fault of the Cadillac, nor even of the rock, but a combination of circumstances added to our burden, as we had assumed responsibility for getting the big black beauty to California in shape. Now we were driving tense from fear of motor muck, and cock-eyed from the shattered windshield. So, leaning tensely to the left, we made New Mexico, where we noticed a broad black trail following us. This was diagnosed as a leak in the oil department, and was followed almost immediately by a leak in our expense money.

You might think that sailing would become smoother as the desert stretched before us, the sun was high, the mountains rose purple out of the plains, and some tumblin' tumbleweeds that we mistook for parts of the Cadillac bounced about the road. But the fates were not done with us. It was in Arizona that an enterprising young filling station attendant checked our tires, and ran his hand through two of them. "If you have a blowout, lady, you'll sure be killed," he warned gravely, "and you'll sure have a blowout." We suggested the spare, and on examining it he found that it was about half the size of a Cadillac tire, and would be a tight fit on a Henry J.

In New Mexico we were arrested a second time, for humming more than eighty miles an hour. It was also in New Mexico that we were forced to purchase the lady truck driver's license, as the authorities at the state line were under the false impression that we were making money on the deal.

Pasadena, the goal, stretched ahead through yet another desert. Rat that we are, we deserted the sinking ship at Phoenix. The girls sailed on and on, like Columbus, and eventually reached the used car lot in California that was their goal. They deposited Black Beauty, said a prayer for some unsuspecting Californian who would pay $3,500 for him, and returned to Phoenix by bus. They were somewhat bedraggled after their bus trip, during which a small Mexican child threw up on Cousin Susan, and Cousin Vicki sat by a young sailor who confided to her that he had a wart on his brain.

The conclusions are clear. If your lot in life is dull and safe, and you yearn to roam, remember the saga of westward the women, and be dull and safe, and be glad.

Pawley's Island

IN THESE CHANGING times it may be noteworthy that there is a small beach resort, four miles long and a quarter of a mile wide, on the upper coast of South Carolina, that flatly refuses to change at all. And the only ripple that disturbs the calm contentment of its summer colony is the ugly rumor, repeated now for several years, that "the developers are coming."

If there is one thing Pawley's Island, South Carolina, does not wish to be, it is "developed." Developed, to Pawley's Islanders, means small cramped houses with plate glass windows unprotected from the sun, air-conditioning, swimming pools and night clubs, neon lights and hot-dog stands, roller coasters and Strangers.

Like Charleston, South Carolina's holy city, Pawley's accepted its set of values a long time ago, and so far as it is concerned, they haven't changed a bit. They have to do with the Atlantic Ocean, with the family, past and present, with the happy hour on the piazza at sunset, with the weathered old summer homes they own or rent year in and year out, with All Saints' Church, Waccamaw, where most of the colony is liable to turn up on Sunday, and strangely enough, with the best places to be buried. More of this later.

You can get to Pawley's from Charleston on U.S. Highway 17, or from Myrtle Beach, its noisy neighbor to the north. From Charleston you cross the Cooper River bridge and drive north to Georgetown. Thence it is just a short sprint to Lachicotte's Store, Pawley's agora and part of its tradition. It was to a Lachicotte that the Gray Man, Pawley's celebrated ghost, first appeared, to ask for supper and warn of a storm. It is alleged that he is still around when needed, though the Islanders continue to maintain good relations with the Coast Guard, too.

At Lachicotte's you turn off the highway, cross a short bridge over a silver-gray creek, and drive into one of the most relaxed summer colonies in the world. The architecture of Pawley's houses can only be described as seventeenth century carpenter. Their style suggests that Mr. Thomas George Pawley, who started the beach resort about one hundred years ago, sent some of his skilled laborers from his rice plantation to his beach property, with the succinct instruction to "put up a house." This they did, with the obvious purpose of making plenty of room for the family, when that term included all "the sisters and the cousins and the aunts."

The houses are leggy structures, built on pilings and surrounded by myrtles and yucca. Weathered silvery by time and the salt air, most of them have porches all around them, so that the family can follow the shifting breeze without a lull in the conversation. One row of houses, including a few guest houses or small inns, fronts on the Atlantic Ocean; a narrow street runs between these and the houses on the tidewater creek which makes Pawley's an island. The guest houses accommodate a small number of select boarders who share the opinion of the regulars that Pawley's is a little bit of heaven between the highway and the sea.

What gives Pawley's its special flavor, of course, are the regulars, people who have been coming to Pawley's since they were children, whose fathers came before them, and who sincerely believe that Pawley's is the most beautiful beach in the world. A late afternoon visit on any porch may well turn out to be an exercise in genealogy, with the old southern game of "Do you know?" thrown in. The regulars know all about each other, and have for years, and nobody has to prove anything to anybody.

Nor do they try, as they go about their restful routine, which includes riding the big waves, watching the sea birds, taking walks over the dunes to the north point of the island, and taking long naps after midday dinners which may include such dishes as gumbo, rice, she-crab soup, broiled flounder, corn on the cob, sliced tomatoes or fresh butterbeans, in prodigal profusion.

She-crab soup is a specialty of the region, and is the Gullah Negroes' name for a South Carolina invention which combines the roe of the female crab with white crabmeat, sherry and the more usual ingredients to produce a cream soup of great distinction. You have to be a very ambitious gourmet, however, to attempt this production yourself, for while any house can provide the children or the cash to get the crabs, the effort involved in getting two cups of white crabmeat and crab eggs is exhausting. After one such experience I conclude that the only underpriced item on the market today is crabmeat, which is surely worth $7.00 a pound if your time is worth anything.

Shrimping in the creek is a delight for the children and the young in heart, who should also be sound of wind and limb to pull the full nets onto the shore and dump their glittering contents on the sand. You must put on sneakers to guard against sharp oyster shells, and then the procedure is to march out into the pluff mud of the creek with your net, seining where the tide is most likely to dump its treasures. The shrimping nets are big affairs, and require at least a two-man or a man-and-child team to operate them. The fascination of this sport is that you always catch *something*. Squid, crabs, baby flounders, eels, and strange prehistoric creatures who have never bothered to crawl out of the mud and evolve, may be in the net, along with the little creek shrimp which are as much a regional favorite as she-crab soup.

In the sunset the piers on the creek, with their peaked wooden roofs, look like Japanese prints. On the ocean side the sunset turns the foaming Atlantic to silver and gold. So there is a running debate about the comparative merits of the views. Sunset, too, brings the happy hour, which involves a cool drink, a hum of talk consisting in large part of family stories, affirmations about the charm of Pawley's, company coming by to say hello, and an occasional slap at a languid mosquito. A strong sense of kin permeates the place, and there may be three or four generations represented on the porch. Pawley's is one of the few places left on earth where the older generation is highly regarded, and this affectionate respect, combined with salt air, may contribute to longevity.

At twelve noon on a summer's day the beach is at its busiest, and this isn't very busy. A pleasant scattering of swimmers, young and old, bounce about in the waves or sit in the sun. A good many family dogs share their owners' enthusiasm for Pawley's, and scamper about the beach, barking at sea birds who dip into the ocean for their dinner. Fishing and surfing equipment may be had at the one public pier on the beach. Youngsters who want to go "out on the town" can play putter golf or jump on the trampoline at the modest recreation center, and teenagers who crave soul music can drive to Myrtle Beach, where the beat goes on.

So that about covers the program at Pawley's as I found it. Sleeping, sunning, swimming, shrimping. Eating often and well. With maybe a cook in the kitchen, if you plan ahead. The Pawley's Island regular cannot imagine wanting to do anything else, or he would not be a regular. But a restless visitor, bound to see some sights, can find plenty to see nearby. He can visit the Hammock Shop, where the famous Pawley's Island hammocks are made by Gullahs and shipped around the world. About ten miles from Pawley's is Hobcaw Barony, where Franklin Roosevelt visited Bernard M. Baruch. Brookgreen Gardens, a "flora and fauna preserve" and sculpture garden established on parts of four old rice plantations by Archer M. Huntington in the 1930s is just a stone's throw, if you are a good thrower. Old Brookgreen plantation, birthplace of Washington Allston in 1779, was used as "Blue Brook plantation" by Julia Peterkin in her Pulitzer Prize winning novel, *Scarlet Sister Mary*. And it was from the Oaks, another Allston plantation now part of Brookgreen Gardens, that Theodosia Burr Allston left for New York to visit her father, Aaron Burr, and was lost at sea.

If you are very ambitious, you can drive to Murrell's Inlet, turn off to a landing on the Waccamaw River, and take the *Island Queen*, an aging motor launch, for a voyage up the Waccamaw and Pee Dee Rivers and look at the water gates on the old rice plantations, and some of the plantation houses that can be seen from the river. It is possible that the *Island Queen* will get stuck in the mud at low tide, but if you wait long enough the tide will rise, and the *Queen* will puff off again on her journey into the past.

Back to the best places to be buried, which I noted as a Pawley's Island conversation topic. When I visited Pawley's Island last, one of our house party announced with great cheer that she had been invited to come "in" to Trinity Churchyard, Columbia. It seems that an invitation to this final resting place is a consummation devoutly to be wished, as exclusive and a good deal more permanent than an invitation to a St. Cecelia Ball. Trinity Churchyard, Columbia, contains all that is mortal, which must be precious little by now, of three Revolutionary soldiers, ten clergymen, three Confederate generals, four governors of South Carolina, three presidents of the University of South Carolina, a bishop, a poet, and a faithful sexton named Pleasant Good.

In the early days of Trinity Parish burial lots were granted to pew-holders. The little churchyard, less than an acre in size, soon filled up, and now one gets invited "in" this Westminster of the Old South only when a hereditary grave-holder forfeits his space.

The churchyard at All Saints', Waccamaw, is also considered a proper final resting place. The congregation was organized in 1767 and its grave stones, shaded by moss-hung oaks, are a history of the rice planters of the low country. Mr. Thomas George Pawley is buried here, and his epitaph predicts the tempo of his island. It reads: "He fell asleep."

Allison's Wells

IT IS HARD for me to realize that Allison's Wells has to be explained, for it was such a special part of Mississippi life in the forties and fifties. The prospect of a weekend at Allison's was enough to sustain me through the week; a thirty-mile drive from Jackson on twenty-five cent gasoline led to another world. There at the end of a winding gravel road off old Highway 51 the rambling resort hotel sparkled in summer with its seasonal coat of white paint, and in the kitchen an ancient black cook produced culinary marvels on a fragrant wood stove. The old well house was a reminder of the magical properties attributed to its healing waters; waters temporarily healing and more palatable were available in the Fishes' Club. The Pavilion was the focal point of constant activity, from snapping beans to painting portraits, and the heart of Allison's was the dining room, dim and cool, where dignified family servants served memorable meals to diners from Jackson, Canton, the Delta, the hills, and metropolitan areas as far away as Memphis. Presiding over the whole production with grace and charm were John and Hosford Fontaine, the hereditary proprietors, who dressed for dinner because dinner was worth dressing for, and expected you to do the same.

Perhaps it should be noted that Allison's Wells was not for everybody. There were and are those who might prefer a Holiday Inn. It is true that at Allison's there was a good deal of uncertainty. Allison's regulars learned to expect the unexpected, and that was part of the fun. For example, it happened upon one occasion that the dreamy youngster at the registration desk assigned two honeymoon couples to the same bedroom. When the Art Colony was in session experimental art might appear mysteriously in the guest rooms, the plumbing was always independent, and for several seasons chicken wire was much in favor for decorating effects. Mattresses and springs varied in quality from room to room, and old friends might be quickly switched from A-grade accommodations to an A-minus room if an A-plus dignitary of church or state hove into view. No matter, this is the stuff conversation is made of, and no planned activities were necessary so long as the guests had the other guests to talk about.

In a laudable effort to cool the dining room one hot Mississippi summer, an ingenious window fan was rigged up, which was supposed to blow through wet straw, thus cooling the air in the dining area and producing an early version of air conditioning. The straw was to be kept wet by a hose, which ran from a tub of water on the porch to the straw packed in the window. On the occasion of a July birthday party, soap bubbles suddenly burst upon the startled diners. At first, the dinner guests were simply amazed. They later compared notes, and reported that they all saw spots before their eyes at the same time. After much slapping at the air, the spots were identified as soap bubbles, which burst impartially into the soup, the salad, and the entree. It seems that the hose had inadvertently been immersed in the laundry tub, thus producing the unexpected visual effects. Was Hosford daunted by this phantasmagoria? Not at all. When a sudsy guest complained she smiled sweetly and said, "Darling, isn't it wonderful? Where but at Allison's could this have happened?"

As has been shown, Hosford was an early exponent of positive thinking. She could be seen any cold morning in early spring or late fall strolling gracefully toward the ice-cold swimming pool, fed by waters which must have originated in a glacier. Without changing pace she would step lightly into the pool, do a few brisk laps, and float out, with never a sign to indicate that the temperature of the water was below freezing. This attitude enabled her to convince newcomers to the spa that shelling peas was fun, darning old table linen an art, and dredging leaves out of the swimming pool a game. Regulars knew better, but all had to serve their apprenticeship.

The ultimate reward for being a good guest was an invitation to "the Retreat." This meant a drink before dinner with John and Hosford in their bosky hideaway beneath their own apartment. A basement space had been screened and floored with bricks; outside a cornfield pressed close, and vines of various denominations clung to the screens. Inside there was candlelight and conversation. If there should be a lull in the conversation, which was unlikely, you might hear an owl hoot or a dove mourn. The Retreat's furnishings were eclectic, and so were the guests. John and Hosford might gather together a collection of artists and writers, clergymen and cotton planters, bridge players and ordinary people, provided they all seemed to be guests of good will. If their will was not good when they entered the retreat, it was usually good when they left. A white-coated waiter brought ice and real napkins, two drinks—no more, no less, were served, tall tales were told, and the stories got funnier with the second drink.

Allison's Wells burned to the ground in 1963, shortly after John's death. John's water colors, Hosford's oils, as well as papers, books, silver, antique furniture, and souvenirs of almost fifty years were lost in the fire. Many of us who belonged to the Allison's enclave lost more than that. We lost a special place that had preserved for us a special time and enhanced our lives.

Autumn Light

ABOUT THIS TIME each year we have a terrific yen to go native. Native Mississippi, that is. So we get in our little gray car and we take a ride. This Sunday we would urge you to do the same, if the autumn sun is out, and we have a tour all planned for you.

Mount your motor and head for the river. The old man himself. At Vicksburg, after driving through flat cotton fields and vine-covered bluffs, take a right on the river road, and head north. On Highway 61 you will pass plantations and cattle farms on the right, backed up to the hills, and on the left will be the level land along the Yazoo River.

On a sunny day in October there is a special autumn light that sifts through the sweet gums and oaks and the shiny pines and turns the fields of broom straw and bitterweed to gold. You will see cattle grazing on the slopes and cotton pickers in the field, trailing their long dun-colored sacks of cotton behind them. If the cotton pickers will accommodate by wearing bright colors, they make a very pretty picture for an itinerant photographer. The cotton wagons, anyway, are dependable. Red and green and blue, and filled to the brim with the staple crop, these high-sided vehicles are largely motorized now, but a searcher for local color will still find a good many Mississippi mules jogging down the road with the wagon clattering behind them.

Along the highway, tiny weathered cotton houses, with vines growing out of them, are brimful of cotton, like popcorn spilling out of a sack. Dog-trot shacks, weathered silver, are rickety in the fields, and now and then a washing machine, proudly anchored to the front porch, denotes a burst of prosperity. The road winds through groves and over a bridge under which the

Yazoo River, flecked with a white frosting of cotton from a nearby gin, flows toward its union with the Mississippi.

At Yazoo City, take 49 to the "wide, flat lands that love and touch the sky," which is to say, Mr. Will Percy's Delta. All the fields are flat now, and you are riding straight through the harvest, past gins and wagons and cotton houses by the highway. You are riding through the historic crop on which Mississippi built her fortunes in the days before diversification, and on which she still depends, to a large degree. The October sun is gentle on the fields, and if you would know what you are about, you will take a long and lingering look, for this is Mississippi as it may be for the last time.

With mechanization the Negro cotton pickers and the cotton houses and the horse-drawn cotton wagons will go, and a phase of regional life will be ended forever. For the warmth and personality and feel of it, you'd better take this ride soon, and hold the Mississippi cotton country in your memory forever, as you see it now, in the autumn light.

DATE DUE

DEMCO 38-297